STREAMLINE SUCCESS:

ELIMINATE CHAOS FROM YOUR SERVICE BUSINESS

ISBN: 9781795899345

Imprint: Independently published

Dedication

To my sons, Giuseppe and Julian.

Rave Reviews

"Streamline Success is more than just a business book; it's a book about life, relationships and helping you build your business. Dorothy doesn't waste time with theories. This book doesn't share knowledge, it inspires action!"

Dr. Gale Carney, Chiropractic Marketing Doctor

"Dorothy takes such a strong charge and initiative in the business environment that she makes everyone around her want to up their game"

Brian R. Boal, CPA, Principal – Boal & Associates PC

"In this book, Dorothy shares what she has learned, both personally and as an entrepreneur. She has grit, persistence and smarts! So many good take-aways and lessons learned for anyone exploring life as an entrepreneur! She demonstrates passion to be successful, no matter what."

Yvonne Campos, Founder Campos Market Research Inc. Founder Next Act Fund - a woman focused angel fund.

"Dorothy has succeeded in a wide variety of endeavors. Her ability to connect with customers is remarkable."

Alan Robertson, Publisher (retired)
Pittsburgh Business Times.

"Dorothy's program has helped me grow personally and professionally, I can't thank her enough!"

Fred Johnson, LMT.

"Dorothy is extremely innovative!"
Leah Laffey, CEO, HealthSouth, Western Pa.

"Dorothy is one of the most impressive people I have ever met. A true leader with team oriented skills, and she is the definition of customer service."
Bill Weissgerber, Principal, Railey Realty.

"Dorothy built her empire with
strength, resilience and stability"
Shea Murtaugh, CEO Hoffmann Murtaugh Media.

Special Thanks

I would like to thank my husband Daryl, for his unyielding support; Michele, Jonelle and Kafi, for their belief in me; my WPO women for all that we are to each other; Colin, for guiding me through the publishing process; John Fenton, for seeing the possibilities in my future; Joel Bauer, for bringing it out; Jeff Faldalen, for showing me the bright side; Mr. Val Zola, for building so many foundations in the beauty industry; my family, staff, friends, mentors, teachers, and shining examples, as well as every female entrepreneur who has gone before me; fearless leaders, who use vision, desire, and courage to propel themselves to the other side.

Table of Contents

Introduction

"We are a product of our decisions,
not our circumstances."

-- Steven Covey

Imagine doubling your company's revenue, building your brand's strength, and attracting the staff and clients you want – all while enjoying more time with your family, your friends, and on hobbies you love. That's what I'd like to share with you in this book.

For thirty-eight years I've been building, branding, succeeding in, and loving the service industry. I've started seven businesses and purchased two others in five different industries. I've forged new markets where they did not previously exist. As I was growing rapidly with some of these companies, I was a single mother with two young sons. At a few points during this time, I was going through extreme personal challenges, changes, grief, and new beginnings.

This book exists for you. Halfway into my career, I started receiving invitations to speak at conferences full of entrepreneurs and community leaders. I stood on stages all over the country, shared my story, and gave suggestions to help the audience start and grow their businesses. Often, after the engagement, a line of people waited to tell me how my stories impacted them. Those people and their positive feedback were the motivation to create this book. I have done my best to include only the tips and strategies which have proved useful for service business owners like you.

Service businesses are not for everyone. We are responsible for employees, customers, and personal growth. Then we go home to manage all the moving parts of our lives at home.

In case you didn't know it, you are a hero. I have a special place in my heart for any person like you, who is courageous enough to start, maintain, and grow a service business. It takes a unique mindset to succeed in the profession you have chosen.

The purpose of this book is to share practical strategies for creating more simplicity and ease in your life. I'll show you how to create more time for high-profit activities, how to hire better people, and (more importantly), keep employees and clients for a lifetime. I'll also share suggestions for increasing your business's revenue, your personal income, and your net worth. You may not agree with everything I suggest. That is okay. Perhaps in disagreeing, you will gain clarity and insight into your own strengths and gifts.

In order to create this book in a way that makes a lasting impact on your life, we will be doing some easy "thinking" exercises. I will ask you a series of questions and suggest you take a couple moments to consider your answers. We will examine how the key areas of life can be improved upon. We will get our priorities in order, separate the time-wasters from the money-makers, and develop guidelines to keep you aligned with the future you want and deserve.

Research on memory-recall has proven that writing with your hand helps gather information and retain it longer. Writing is a critical part to help you define the facets of business and life you want. If you keep your ideas in your thoughts, they usually drift away. So, I recommend you write some of your thoughts down too. You will be the only person who sees your writing.

Following the structure of the book in a linear way, from beginning to end, will likely be more effective than jumping around. I've designed it to flow in an order of importance, as the stages you will go through to eliminate chaos and create joy.

We'll start with a simple understanding of what brought you to this point, and then delve into managing ourselves, our time, and situations as we grow in the chaotic world of the service industry.

Part One: Create Your Vision

Why do some people slog through life miserably, while others feel a sense of ever-expanding joy and satisfaction?

What causes one business person to prosper while another, in the same industry and economy, shuts their doors and gives up?

How do we ensure our happiness and accomplishment?

I believe the answer to all those questions comes down to our personal *vision* of the future.

For years, people have told me that I make my businesses look effortless. However, the reality is quite the contrary. I've worked hard and overcame more obstacles than almost any other business owner I've known. The truth is, unbeknownst to me, I was doing exactly what I wanted to do in every company, charity, endeavor, and organization I've been involved with. I stayed on track with a clear personal vision of the future. I set my intention from the beginning, to play by my own set of rules, be aware and respectful of those around me, provide safe employment, and create abundant opportunities for those who want them.

So, how do we create a compelling vision? The process sounds simple: choose the future we want, and then reflect on which parts of our past are useful to create that future. Ah, if it were only this easy. We will look at how chaos corrupts the 'ease' part of that equation.

Designing your vision starts in this present moment. I can't count the amount of times a coach or speaker has asked: "When you were a child, what did you aspire to become?" That question is useful only after you've looked at your future first. Who cares what you wanted when you were six, or eight, or ten? That's in the past! You are where you are, right now. You are brand new in this present moment, with the power to create the future you want.

The Future Starts Now

Of your desires, which are the most important to you today? What are some of your biggest dreams and ideals? Even if you could never imagine accomplishing these dreams within your lifetime, when you do think about them, what makes you feel motivated and inspired?

Knowing what we want from life, allows us to create it. When we cannot *see* something in our future, it is virtually impossible to fulfill. By clearly defining our vision and imagining that which does not yet exist, only then, can we stand in that future and be fully immersed in what we want, and understand how we want it. How it looks, how it feels, how it impacts our time, our clients, and our family, as well as how it impacts our community; the more clearly we see it, the easier our road is.

When I start creating my next big idea, I approach it in one of two ways. This is an important piece I'm consciously aware of. When I'm working hard to visualize the steps, the cost, the people involved, and the specific outcome I want to arrive at, it feels laborious. When I let it simmer and it's still difficult to piece together, my idea is off the mark. I kiss it goodbye, knowing it was a great exercise to rule this one out. My creative thought-process has protected me from a potential mistake. I always trust this process.

In contrary and always in response to a problem, when I'm on to the right train of thought, it flows easily. The ideas come in spades. They rush in, sometimes in a matter of minutes. The entire high concept is there. When this happens, I act. Pay attention when that happens to you. It is the gift of your thoughts aligning with who you are meant to be.

Let's assume as an example, you feel it's time to change something about your career. At first you're not certain what it is, but your inner voice is nagging at you to move on, to find motivation, to provide, and to create. Then you notice you've recently started paying attention to things you look forward to; a particular problem, or an absence of something that would be convenient.

For this exercise, let's say you need to drive fifty minutes across town to the craft beer bar you've been telling your friends about. You love visiting this taproom. You love what they provide. You feel great every time you're there with friends. You wished they served more casual food, and they could be closer to your own neighborhood.

The next week, you notice an old gas station is going out of business near your home. It's a great location in a busy neighborhood. When it occurs to you that a craft beer bar, which serves tapas and has an open mic night, would be the ideal business for this spot, you realize you might be on to something. How do you know? It all flows through your mind quickly. You can visualize it clearly. When you find yourself sitting on the bench across the street from the gas station, imagining what a new space could look like, you're creating your future business.

For some people, the dream dies there. Their inner voice tells them they can't think that big and it is a dream for someone else. But for the entrepreneur at heart, you pay attention to the excitement you feel. You find yourself looking for craft beer-making classes. You start asking around the neighborhood about rent, parking, and the bus schedule that could bring employees to work. You get into bed that night and the feeling is still there. You let it "brew," literally, in your mind, as you drift off to sleep.

The next morning, you start writing a plan of attack. You call a leasing agent, and a friend who owns a bar in another town, to ask questions and gather information. You write, you call, and you visualize. You take action.

Taking action is what separates the doers from the dreamers.

Nine months later, you are celebrating your grand opening. The four employees you hired and trained are serving beer flights and small plates of food to a roomful of people who appreciate this new venue. You invited a friend who sings like Adele, to bring her boyfriend and his guitar to cover the 9:00 p.m. hour. People are swaying in their seats.

You stand back physically exhausted, yet emotionally energized, somewhat afraid, but full of hope, joy, and passion. You cannot wait to come back and unlock the door tomorrow. You have taken control of your happiness, finances, and your future. You are providing employment for awesome people who share your vision. You, my friend, have started a service business!

You will hear at least three people say over the first few weeks, "I was thinking about opening a craft beer bar too." These are the people whose dreams died on their couch, while your dream processes their credit cards.

Our past dreams and desires are useful for creating a positive future, only once we have a clear idea of what we want. Our past can give us a sense of motivation and inspiration to create that future. Hidden skills, talents, and abilities could be lying dormant from your "childhood self." As a result of clarifying your future vision, you're now in a perfect position to utilize those talents and abilities from your past.

Which Part of Your Past Will Help You Now?

What decisions did you make as a young person that were hard, nearly impossible, but served you well at the time? Be patient, there is a reason we are going back to our youth here.

At some point, usually in early childhood, something important happened to us and we made a subconscious decision.

If you're a child who stays up late watching movies with a parent, you know the more you engage about the movies, the more time and attention you get from this parent. You've made a decision to be astute regarding movies. By the time you're in high school, you and your dad can quote favorite lines from movies you enjoyed together. It would not be surprising if you turned out to be a filming, editing or video specialist in your adult life.

The opposite is true when we have early failures. When we are not able to keep up with our peers, our siblings, or our schoolmates in certain areas, we start avoiding them altogether.

As a child, I was slightly scrawny. During the summer, kids on my street often picked teams for street games like relay races, tag, or whiffle ball. I can still remember hearing them say, "She's too slow, she's too skinny," etc. I decided I couldn't be good at sports and therefore, I sat on my porch and read while my neighbors played. Occasionally I would join in, but I always knew I would never be winning any of those contests.

This *"already always"* expecting to win or lose, as a subconscious thought pattern, determines in large part, where we end up.

It took years to overcome my insecurities about sports. As an adult, I still tend to shy away from group activities such as volleyball. Non-contact activities that include only a few people at a time are more in sync with my comfort level. We think these types of attractions and fears are 'just the way we are' but how we are is actually rooted in the decisions we made as children.

Can you recall a few decisions you made as a child?

- Do you see how they have helped you succeed?
- Do you see how they have held you back?

How Our Past
Can Impact Our Future

During early high school, I felt rudderless. I wasn't sure what I wanted to do with my future. My surroundings were somewhat limiting.

I decided to change my primary group of friends when I was getting into some things that were over my head. I wanted to keep my current friends; I loved them, yet I wanted to avoid activities that could potentially cause trouble. It was hard balancing this shift as a teenager without much parental support. I couldn't discuss this angst with friends. Instead, I followed my gut feelings and made changes, hoping to make money cutting hair.

I got involved in hairstyling, immersing myself in a world that was foreign to every friend I had. Doing that expanded my circle of friends. I had to enroll in the local Vo-Tech school, which was not the beacon of scholarly honors, but it felt right, and I could get in if I had two years of Algebra. I was tutored for the rest of my sophomore year in Algebra, and then got accepted to the Cosmetology program. Algebra never came easy to me, until I viewed it as a stepping stone to get what I really wanted: a new future.

Making this change was the beginning of what would be a big and bright future in the beauty profession. This was not my intention; I just didn't want to drop acid on Friday nights.

I've watched intelligent and talented individuals lose jobs and companies as a result of their addictions. We cannot make concise choices when we impair our brains and numb our thought process. If we've been raised in an environment where drugs and alcohol are used to manage stress, we may self-medicate when we feel pressure. This is a part of our past that limits our future.

We all have things that happen in our lives that shape us. They may feel subtle at the time, but looking back, we can clearly see these changes. We all have those stories. Without them we would not be able to grow up. When we're young, we rarely think of or look at life that way. It is only as we grow both in age and emotional awareness that we realize we need to stop ignoring the strengths we have, and start mining for their gold. That is a highly individual process.

I present my story to show you that our current reality is no accident. Breaking the *belonging pattern* is one of the most difficult things we can do. Foraging for new friends is hard. This process builds strength and skills that carry us far in life.

We have crafted our life to get to this point. As a child, I wanted to be a Catholic Nun, then an artist, and then a physical therapist. These dreams were all useful desires, even if their only purpose was to guide me in a different direction. As Marshall Goldsmith said, and even titled one of his many excellent business books, *What Got You Here Will Not Get You There.*

Prepare for Adversity

Once we've gained more emotional clarity by understanding past beliefs, as well as who holds us back, it is easier to see which direction to move toward. The path to get there is never a straight arrow upwards. Our personal conviction is often tested.

Sure, as my career was building, there was chaos, miserable days, and crisis looming around every corner. There were setbacks so large that I wanted to hide under the bed for fear of incoming missiles – but it's how we respond that defines our character. Deeply challenging and miserable situations are what teach us the most in life.

Leaders need strength, thick skin, and determination. We need empathy and understanding. We need to step in and work when we've had no sleep or food, and do it all with a smile. We rarely offer excuses. We refill our own fuel tanks on the fly.

Determined? Afraid? Anxious? Self-doubting? No support system? Money challenges? Big Dreams?

Yes, you are right where you should be.

There is not a person I know, who started a new endeavor without a degree of trepidation. Even when we are certain we're doing the right things, fear and hesitation are part of the process. We are not alone in questioning ourselves, our capabilities, our choices, and our actions. This is one of the ways we constantly check ourselves.

When we feel fear creeping up, be on the alert. It's our spirit telling us there is something to pay attention to. Work through the thoughts, look at your options, and be prepared for roadblocks, obstacles, and flying matter to come in to view. If it was easy, anyone could do it.

Giving into fear can shut us down. Each case is individual, but the best way I've found to get through gripping fear, is to look back at what I've accomplished to date. I keep a hand-drawn timeline on the wall in front of my desk, with my major hurdles and accomplishments. This exercise reminds me that I have solved problems before, and will solve them again. Consider that same type of journal for yourself.

It is not a sign of weakness to say, "I'm not sure. Let me think about it." We do not need to have all the answers. Our vulnerability is a point of power. When we pretend to know something we don't, it is apparent. I'm not talking about taking risks in new areas that we are unsure of. I'm talking about not having an answer or a solution for a specific question or problem.

When this happens, you have choices. You can discuss the situation in an open forum. Some leaders don't like doing this; they fear it makes them look weak. If this sounds familiar, you might want to look into how controlling you are in situations.

When we need to gather more information to arrive at a conclusion, it's a sign of confidence to say, "I want to learn more before I take us in a particular direction." By doing this, we're teaching our team to be thoughtful and thorough when making decisions. Taking the pressure away from ourselves is our job. No one else may recognize or care that we feel internally overwhelmed. When we know this, we are prepared with the courage it takes to protect ourselves.

When forging a new market, there is a lot of uncertainty. Relying on our own instincts is critical. Arming ourselves with the best information available is critical. Spending our time with people who are creative thinkers and skilled problem solvers is critical.

Avoiding individuals who sabotage our confidence is also critical. There are times when breaking up from past friends leads us to a more supportive group of people with like-minded desires. Implementing this break in relationships is something we need to do at various points of inflection. Don't feel guilty. Handle it gracefully.

Respecting our own limitations and others', keeps us from being disappointed.

It is a myth that the owner, president, CEO or founder of a company, must have all the answers. If this were truly the case, there would be no room for others in any organization.

Surrounding ourselves with dynamic, creative, intelligent people increases our probabilities for success. Taking what we learn from others' teachings, and delivering it back to our team in a succinct way, is as effective a tool as delivering our own brilliant idea.

Relax, learn, and be open to new ideas. When a leader comes across as calm, the chaos greatly diminishes. Arrange your thoughts, and then share what you want the end results to look like. It's a basic and simple process for internal growth. It doesn't matter what level of education, experience, or success we have.

Complexity keeps inching up right behind us.

It pushes us to be uncomfortable.

It pushes us to become better.

It pushes us to get to the other side.

The other side is where you belong!

Part Two:
Create Balance

Mastering the
Five Keys of Life Balance

It's almost impossible to start, grow, and maintain a business, especially in the service sector, without major impact on every area of our life. Many people think they will compartmentalize their business from the rest of their life, but it really doesn't work this way.

The most important things we do as we grow our company, often have nothing to do with the actual business and everything to do with our attitude, and how we juggle all of it. When our personal life, health, happiness, and family are operating free from chaos, our business flows much easier. When things are spinning wildly out of control, everything suffers.

I've found there are five areas of life that create a sense of balance and organization. I call them the *Five Keys of Life Balance*. These five areas contribute to our happiness and satisfaction. We will look at, discuss, embrace, and educate ourselves about these five areas. The more consciousness we place on these areas will ensure we are not leaving anything on the table when it comes to the depth of happiness we can achieve in our lives. The five areas are:

1. PHYSICAL BEING
2. RELATIONSHIPS
3. SPIRITUAL NEEDS
4. CAREER CHOICES
5. FINANCES

For years, I have been living by and teaching the importance of these five elements. I have shared them with my family, my staff, my clients, my audiences, and my friends. When we shortchange one of these areas, or think we've got it covered and stop working on it, things start falling apart.

Most of us are concerned that we do not have the time, money, energy, or physical and emotional strength to do this. I promise you, it is easier and more implementable than you may think. Find the formula that works for you. Create it, live it, and use it! Life is different for all of us. What my image of an ideal life looks like will always be different from yours.

Let's start with Physical Being, as this piece allows us to do the other components. Plus, without health and strength nothing else works. Our well-being is paramount to our successful future.

MASTERING YOUR PHYSICAL BEING

Our physical state is as much an attitude, as it is a function of activities. First and foremost, we must understand *why* we want to live a long and healthy life. If you aren't clear on this, taking care of yourself becomes less important. If we don't give ourselves something positive to look forward to each day, week, month, year, decade, then the importance of physical health becomes irrelevant because we see no need for its place in our life.

It's easier to see personal disregard in others, than it is to see the behavior in ourselves. The key here is not focusing on the negative. Instead, we want to give ourselves new reasons that drive our choices to eat, think, and act differently. These new actions help us achieve our goals without the need for assisted living conditions in older years, if we can avoid it.

We start by taking an honest look at what we're doing today and then what needs to change. We also want to make sure our change is attainable; it's something we can manage.

Many people stop, fail, or ignore their health program because they have developed a subconscious attitude that they are not worth it. When we have a deep love and respect of ourselves, we are compelled to take care of our body.

When we carry deep shame, guilt, remorse, fears, mistrust of life and love, it's impossible to focus on optimal care of ourselves. Getting to the root of physical manifestations can be challenging because we need to confront ourselves. The goal is to feel safe in loving and respecting ourselves. Then, make a specific plan to manifest that love and respect in the real world. No one else can or will ever do this for us.

- What are three things you are doing now, that if you slowed or stopped would positively impact your body?
- Are you able to visualize your life if you don't take those actions?
- Have you chosen the correct motivating factors to keep you invested in better health?

Make Improvement Easier

We make change easier by breaking it down into manageable steps. After the first small step, we gain confidence to up the ante.

After a lifetime of mostly healthy eating and high activity, I found myself regressing. We recently opened a restaurant, where I spent fifty hours a week working for several months. I was trying to get the company culture correct, while dealing with personal issues. Over the course of three years I gained eighteen pounds. Disgusted that no diet was working and my clothes no longer fit, yoga pants and long sweaters became my outfit of the day. I was stuck.

For those three years, I would wake up every few days and tell myself "today is the day! I'll eat better and get on the treadmill for fifteen minutes." By 8:00 a.m., I was too busy, and the leftover pie on the counter was the quickest thing to satisfy my panic mode hunger.

I was frustrated. I wasn't seeing the progress we needed in the new business, trying to build a stronger leadership team, while neglecting my other company. I felt like the devil was climbing the walls in my own house. From the outside, no one would have known this. My life looked wonderful to most people around me. While I pushed myself to meet deadlines, goals, and expectations, my body was suffering.

After getting blood work that showed flags on all important numbers, I decided it was time to recalibrate my metabolism. I went on a strict twenty-one day no carb, high (good) fat, fiber and protein, ketogenic food program. I mean strict! No wine for several weeks! I joined the local Y, bought new gym shoes, and spent ten minutes every morning doing basic and simple stretches, starting while I was still in bed. While I waited for my coffee to brew, I did fifteen squats in my pajamas. In twenty-one days, I lost fifteen of the pounds. This motivated me to buy some new clothes and makeup. I also cleaned my closets and removed the guilty reminders of items that were now too big, or wasted money spent to soothe myself in a time of hurt.

What really happened was that I forced myself to envision how I wanted to spend the rest of my life. Not being able to pull my jeans up felt humiliating. If I have thirty to forty years left on this earth, I want to maximize those years. When my kids were young, I worked out to keep up with them. Now I do things for myself. This is a hard concept for most of us to grasp. Until we do, we only hurt ourselves. I understand how it feels to let it all go and the gritty determination to get it back.

Pulling ourselves out when we're slacking is always easier when we ask *why* it is important to be better to ourselves. I expect my body to last as long as my brain functions. The vision of my sons changing my diapers in a nursing home is a horrifying notion. My "*why*" is a vision of me chasing around my future grandchildren.

We're all experts at doing what we want while ignoring what we should, because it avoids pain and offers instant gratification. Paying attention to our insights is a gift. Please pay attention to the almost inaudible voice that tells you: "This is not good for me."

When we journal, it helps us become more aware of our patterns. For many years, I did a brief journal every day. This was easier when we had pocket paper calendars and

Day Planners. I'd simply jot a few notes each day. It would take no more than a quick glance at my week to see I was only fooling myself in certain areas of life. The trick here is to find what inspires you to take care of yourself.

Know Your Health KPIs

Successful corporations use KPIs (Key Performance Indicators) as a basis for improving revenue and efficiency. In the same way, we can know our bodies KPIs as a way to keep score of our health. Knowing our baseline is the only way to properly measure our success once we set a goal for ourselves.

I won't go into technical detail, but here is a quick list of health checks we should know about: A1C, HDL, LDL, PSA, and blood pressure. A great place to start would be to schedule an appointment with your doctor and get those tests done. You must know where you're starting from in order to know how far you need to go.

One visit to one doctor and one blood screening could save your life. If you're thinking you want to skim over this part because it doesn't apply to you, then *you* might need the tests the most. We're never too young, too thin, too busy, or too clairvoyant to understand our bodies and what we need to give them in order for them to function properly.

For some of us, taking daily vitamins might be a step in the right direction. For those with specific chronic or genetic situations like diabetes, eliminating your morning bagel with jelly and replacing it with an egg or complex carbohydrate like steel cut oatmeal, might be the simple gift you give yourself and your family.

Genetic diseases need specific care. Recently I was helping a friend, a type 2 diabetic, get into her car. She had a long drive ahead, so snacks to keep her sugar levels steady were important. What I saw was a bag full of mini candy bars and cans of diet soda in the console. Either it never occurred to her, or she simply felt immune to the effects of poor eating which were taking a toll on her prescription log and hospital stays. This sounds crazy, but this denial happens in a majority of chronic cases.

I've heard statements like, "at this point in my life, I don't have to eat what I don't like." For people who have spent their whole lives convincing themselves they are right, it is hard and sometimes impossible to overcome. This is challenging if we are the caretaker as a result of their neglect. Sometimes we take better care of our cars and cats than we do of our bodies. Our body truly is *our* temple.

As a business owner or manager, you know how much energy is needed every day at all levels. We work countless hours. Days off are coveted. Mental stress of overseeing all capacities and responsibilities for the safety, profit, growth, and joy based around our endeavors, is so high it is obsessive. Entrepreneurs live by their own clocks. There is no such thing as 9-5. We do whatever it takes, wherever it is needed. If you don't maintain your strength and health, your business suffers. When I'm on the treadmill, the only way I keep myself there is by putting a work project in my head. I think through how I will handle it, run scenarios and make my plan. Twenty minutes later, I'm sweating, ready to shower and tackle my project. Please find your plan.

Health Culture in Your Company

Preventative measures are characteristics of a leader. Creating a culture where health and wellness are important, shows your team you care personally for their well-being. They feel more in relationship with each other when they have work partners to help support those ideals.

Full-time employees have approximately one hundred and four days each year to spend extra time on their physical goals. This doesn't mean ignoring their health on the other two hundred and sixty-one days. Some employees work long, unpredictable, and tedious hours, especially in the service industries. I believe in creating a culture of health. I don't push my beliefs on my employees. However, in team meetings we make a point to have health as a category for employees to improve upon.

In my experience, employees who have healthy routines, as well as relaxing time off, tend to be higher performers. They have something to look forward to. They come back to work with their batteries recharged.

Movement gives us more energy than coffee ever could. Although coffee is great and I love it, it is America's number one addiction.

In order to move forward with your company's physical plan, look for *three negative things* you could as a group, stop or give up right now, that would benefit the health and longevity of your staff.

- Are these behaviors easy to give up?
- Is the staff willing to participate?
- Will you see measurable results?

As a group, discuss what benefits will occur as a result of the changes. Remember, focusing on the 'why' is where the buy-in starts. Sweeping changes last for less than eight hours. Being unrealistic will cause immediate failure and snorting behind your back. Positivity among staff is as important as physical health.

When things start feeling low, have everyone share what they admire about each other. Practical changes, where staff all feel like they have a part in the decision making process, always leads to a better result. Good group follow up helps keep everyone more aware of their positive outcomes.

Create Constant Reminders

At first it might be a daily glance at the page you bookmark, and then it may be a weekly reminder in your calendar. If you find it easier, then get a partner, friend, or accountability partner to help keep you on track with your health goals. Prepaying for classes, memberships, and training, tends to make us actually show up.

When I'm making a change in anything I'm doing, most especially around food or exercise commitments, I announce it to those I see frequently. My husband knows when I'm carb counting. He stops buying me donuts. He shows me he loves me by purchasing Avocados. My managers are now aware I will be available slightly later two days each week so I can get to spin class. They support what's important to me because I support what's important to them. Physical well-being is a lifelong journey that starts with one small step.

In the 1970s, sneaker companies tried to make us believe if we weren't running five miles a day, we were inadequate. Watching movies from this era, the style was to wear running suits, striped tube socks, and sweat bands as fashion accessories. Then came the 80's, and if we weren't flash dancing with leg warmers in Aerobics classes, we were lazy. Every decade has its prized trend.

Health trends come and go. If you like them, do them. If you don't like them, don't. Please do not judge yourself if your friends have more steps than you at the end of the day. Find what works for you, make it fun, make it regular, and make choices that are in alignment for your best self.

A dear friend, Dr. Will Clower, author of *The Fat Fallacy*, shared with me how eating real food, eliminating processed foods, and adopting more European food habits, not only tastes better, it costs less and helps our body function more efficiently. His theory was proven when he moved his entire family to France and adopted the regional cuisine. Everyone became more fit with improved health.

A few years ago, I heard Dr. Daniel Amen say, and I remember his quote, when walking past the bakery to the vegetable section, *"Food is medicine or food is poison."*

In the 1980's, I was introduced to the teachings of Louise Hays. Her book, *"You Can Heal Your Life,"* changed mine. As I started doing affirmations with myself, little nagging health issues cleared up. Now, thirty years later, I believe that physical ailments are manifestations of emotional strains, or a deep need to belong to our family of origin. I do not discount medical problems or conditions. I just believe there's something else going on.

Celebrate long and prosperous years with the healthy choices you gift to yourself each and every day. This intention will make a positive difference in your life.

MASTERING YOUR RELATIONSHIPS

"The most important decision we make in our life is who we will spend it with."

Why do relationships in every category start out so charming, so full of possibilities, and then go awry. I remember as a child, seeing the front cover of the National Enquirer. It showed Loni Anderson and Eric Estrada on half of the cover, from nine months earlier, espousing their love and adoration for each other. The other half of the cover was the current week. They were calling each other terrible names. They now hated each other. That caused me to question, "Did they change? Did they pretend to be someone else to snare the famous movie star of the moment?"

These questions are, in part, what I've spent the last thirty years examining. Learning about human behavior and how it affects us in relation to the people in our lives. I've spent thousands of hours in one-on-one conversations with people who sat in my chair and intimately opened up about their lives. A salon is a vulnerable, yet oddly safe and slightly anonymous place to share our juiciest stuff. Deep down, we're all the same. We are afraid, we are proud, and we cover up our failures. We try again and we defend ourselves to the ninth degree. We all want to be loved and accepted for who we really are. Yet, we cannot earn this love and acceptance if *we* are blind to or in denial of who we see in the mirror.

As entrepreneurs or high-level managers, our primary relationships fit into two categories: personal and business. I'd like to explore some stories, ideas, and questions that can help you create more healthy and dynamic relationships within both categories. The smoother your relationships function, the better your business runs.

Personal Relationships

Your Spouse/Partner

I opened this section with the following quote: "The most important decision we make in our life is who we will spend it with." My friend Mel said that to me while we were enjoying dinner at our friend Kate's restaurant at Deep Creek Lake, in Western Maryland. Mel and I met several years before, both from Pittsburgh. He's a successful businessman. He has a fabulous wife and family. His daughters are friends with my sons. He is one of the few from our large group of business-oriented friends, who is still married to the original spouse.

Our personal and primary relationships have great impact and significance on how our company operates. I've met wives who have no understanding of how their husbands' businesses function. They raise the kids, spend money, and wonder why they've been cut off from a part of their partner's life. I've known wives who work their fingers to the bones, while their husbands can't figure out what to do for dinner. Their support comes from outside of the home, which brings in a feeling of emptiness. This leads to bigger issues, while the cycle of non-communication circles the drain.

Anne DeVaughn, a leading family therapist and highly respected in her field, says this: *"Couples who have or create common interests and share the interests together, have the most successful marriages I have seen."*

It is true. When one spouse spends inordinate hours of free time doing something their partner has no interest in, it can cause resentment. Finding common ground and enjoying time together helps improve all relationships that are important to us.

When a relationship isn't serving us well, with zero evidence things will change, the best thing we can do is end it gracefully and responsibly. Staying in an unfulfilling relationship is abdicating our power to the other person. If we see there is no room for repair or growth, we must ask ourselves why we are still there. This answer usually involves children, affordability, fear of being alone, asset division, or family attachment.

It's never easy to end a significant relationship. Ideally, we would learn how to communicate and show respect in the way our partner needs to have it delivered. But this takes time, maturity and patience. If you have a great relationship, treasure every minute of your success, with unbridled enthusiasm. If you have a lukewarm lover, take the initiative to improve, through communication whenever possible. There is a reason you chose this person in the first place.

Being in a relationship with an entrepreneur can be tricky. It's not necessarily that our company comes first, but it feels like this to others. Unless they know what it means to be responsible for other people's paychecks and livelihoods, it is hard to understand our level of commitment and loyalty to our company.

When my children were very young, their father and I had a marriage that was lacking the level of depth we both wanted. We made a mutual agreement to have a successful divorce. We parted as friends, and still are to this day. We agreed to never speak or imply a negative word about each other.

Children believe they are made up of half and half of their parents. If they're taught that one parent is a bad person, they innately believe they are half bad themselves. This creates a lifetime of overcoming shame that is unnecessary. Our sons thank us for maintaining a loving family, with the two of us co-parenting our children, positively, lovingly, and respectfully, from separate homes.

Our mutual agreement, allowed us to live the lives we wanted to live. We created a new kind of parental intimacy – the pride of knowing we were making our divorce work for our whole family. We both found at times, this concept was challenging for others to understand. If we were dating someone who couldn't grasp our parameters, that relationship usually didn't last long. Our extended families both consider us a part of the family, because we are, by the relation to their two grandsons, nephews and cousins (our sons).

Dating, as an entrepreneur can be tough. I was selfish about my time with my sons and time for my business. I recall a date complaining, as we were heading to my condo near one of my businesses for a long weekend, that I spent the first twenty minutes of the drive on the phone with a manager.

I thought for a minute, he is an employee - he has no idea what it takes. I explained that if I ignored the issue and didn't take the manager's call, not only would I be irresponsible, but my chances of free time as the day went on, would be decreased.

Not many people new to a relationship with an entrepreneur can be as understanding as we need them to be. I've been in relationships with other entrepreneurs. It is unspoken, company crisis trumps cocktails and dinner plans.

At a point early in the formation of The Sewickley Spa, I was in a serious relationship with a brilliant marketer. I asked for his help with creating my first advertising campaign. When he saw the success I was having, he asked if he could join my company.

Not fully understanding what I was entangling myself into; I gifted him stock in exchange for his consulting. However, I was deeply emotionally connected to this man and missed his personal agenda. Within the course of the next two years, my life became a personal hell. When we are in it, we cannot see it.

Sparing many details, I almost lost my company.

The separation process was grueling. When I learned he was funneling our revenue into a credit card processing account he created by forging my name, in Ohio, I had the leverage I needed to remove him. I was not graceful, I was not elegant. I was desperate. My mother's nursing home bills loomed over me, my children needed my attention, and my staff needed their jobs. It cost a large sum of money, my pride, and an expensive lesson about involving a personal relationship into my professional life. That made me stronger. I would never have been able to overcome future incredible hurdles, had I not walked through this particular fire.

There's a difference between supportive power shifts, and ones based on control. Power needs to balance between a couple, shifting as situations change. When one person controls power too long it creates a one-sided dynamic and weakens the couple as a whole. When power shifts from one side to the other, the bond strengthens, and trust develops.

It is only through navigating intense adversity, that strong character is built. Difficult primary relationships provide us an immense appreciation for what a high honor, trusting relationship looks and feels like. I don't view my past relationships as failures. I view them as opportunities for growth.

For each relationship that ends, we cheat ourselves by not looking at our part in the problems. If you've experienced false starts or "kissed a couple of frogs," I guarantee you are better off focusing on the positive lessons you learned. Focusing on shortcomings of the person who will be a part of your past is a time-wasting activity.

If you're in a relationship now with a spouse and you are happy, congratulations! Make sure you take time to show him/her, how important they are to you.

In order to have the supportive relationship I now have with my husband, I had to give up everything I knew about how a relationship should work. We make it work for us. It is fluid and it changes daily. We adjust. We make an effort to show each other that we are a priority above all else. The effort is worth the return, even when it is the smallest of gestures. In regard to your intimate relationships, consider for a moment the following questions:

- Is this relationship meeting my needs?
- Do I feel special to my partner?
- Am I motivated to make my partner feel special?
- Do we both value transparency and honesty?
- Do I demonstrate clearly to my partner how happy they make me?

If we hide things from our partner, there's a problem. Either we don't understand what it means to have healthy relationships, or there is a lack of trust between the couple. Getting external attention can be intoxicating. Deleting messages so a partner doesn't see what we discuss with someone else, is a death wish on any relationship. Learning why this type of attention is necessary will empower you for the rest of your life. This kind of attraction diverts attention away from personal growth at most every level.

In the end, making bad decisions only hurts us and undermines our character. Affairs, often prevalent with people in the service industry, take years of hard work to recover from. The passionate part of our personality that leads us to run highly exciting companies is the same passion that can lead us into relationship trouble.

- Are you prepared for accepting partnership growth and change that is inevitable as you and your company grow and change?

Once we fully commit to another human being, they must be viewed as the best option for us at every turn. Intentionally creating our partner as the most interesting, sexiest, fun, and creative person we will ever know, keeps it alive. If you cannot shift your thinking, you may be tempted by the fruits of another in the future.

In order to fully appreciate what and who you have, make it a daily habit to remember the things that made you fall in love with this person in the beginning. Focusing on our partner's positive attributes causes them to show up differently. *They* actually never changed: *we* changed. We changed where we put our attention and energy.

We tend to use the diversion of our company as a distraction from working through issues in personal relationships. Some of us thrive on a great relationship to help support the outpouring of energy we give to others. Some of us are single and thrive on the freedom to work as much as we want to. There is no right or wrong here, only a quest for our own happiness that flows into all other areas of life.

Relationships with Our Children

Quoting Khalil Gibran, the famous philosopher and author of one of my favorite books, *The Prophet*: *"live with your children, not through your children."* Nurture their little personalities. If we're critical of their small steps, they will rebel. Nurturing and discipline are both critical components of parenting. Young children understand far more than we give them credit for. If our three year old toddler is screaming in a tug of war, they didn't learn this on their own. When we scream at our children, we only scare them. Talking slowly and firmly, allowing them to understand they have some sense of control over themselves and the situation creates a sense of calm and trust between parent and child. This can be difficult when we are tired and stressed. But we need to demonstrate emotional responsibility to our children.

When we're afraid to appropriately discipline our children for doing wrong because we want them to love us more, how could they ever learn how to discipline themselves as they grow up?

Positive change happens once we alter our course and focus on the amazing attributes our young child has within themselves. Doing this while helping them to understand why it's bad to bite, push, hit, steal, or bully, results in kids who can hold their own as they grow.

When our children are young, it's an exhausting blur of getting through days and nights. The time goes by so quickly. Getting everyone operating on your daily routine, helps tremendously.

It occurred to me one day as I was doing laundry while Julian, my youngest son, was playing next to me in the laundry room that I only hated laundry because I said so. I decided to be more engaged and turned laundry into a joint experience. I taught him colors, spelling, counting, and pairing. Laundry became a game that day.

I also gave myself a mantra that day. "If it's not fun, I can't do it." We must find the fun in our tasks, or we become negative and resentful while doing them. Our kids emulate our behavior and our upsets, in their desire to be more like us, hoping it makes us like them more.

Involving children in our business is a great gift. We help them develop a sense of family pride. Children see things purely, without the same emotion we bring into situations.

Throughout life, my sons have been my sounding board for business decisions. When Giuseppe was nine, I had a perplexing situation. While recounting this with a friend who joined us for dinner, he inserted his comment into the conversation and it was perfectly, brilliantly, the answer. At that moment, I realized how much exposure they had from birth, about the business world.

To this day, I call my sons when I need to reason through a problem. They listen intently, show me alternative ways to look at things, and give me unbiased answers. Involving our kids in our company enhances their knowledge base with subjects they will never learn in school.

Do you see ways to involve your children in your business? Stuffing envelopes? Sorting ideas on a whiteboard? Helping to name marketing campaigns? Giving fresh ideas on current trends when we get stale?

Julian pointed out as he was folding laundry at the spa, that our towels were 'really ugly'. He was seven years old. I asked the staff if they thought we needed a better quality towel. They overwhelmingly agreed. Children are honest. Listen to their opinions, and thank them for being so astute. The more we praise our challenge, the better they perform. Life is short, fill it with love.

Celebrate millennials: we created them!

Family of Origin

We develop beliefs based on chaos, calm, control, and general behavior, according to what our parents or primary caregivers demonstrated. We make decisions that affect our entire lives; good and bad. Some people believe they act a certain way because it is "in our blood". The reality is, if our blood were transfused into a neighbor with different parents, they would never act like us. When we have unresolved issues with a family member, those problems affect our current relationship with others.

I was born into a family as the unexpected final child. I resented my father's lack of love, attention, and support.

He had a generous and gracious personality, except with me. On the night he was dying, his final words were a negative comment about my appearance. I was twenty-one years old at that time.

I smugly thought and spoke about him with the same disregard, as if I one-upped him by being brash. Yet, deep in my heart, I was hurt. It never occurred to me that I was holding onto subconscious trauma, or that I could reframe my perspective into something positive.

Six years after his death, I enrolled into a *Landmark Education* workshop. I faced how much I was limiting myself with this negativity. Only then, did I have the power to change it. I reinvented my story to say, "My father had a much higher standard for me. He just didn't live long enough to see me realize the potential I had."

My new story, true or not, allowed me to look at my father not as my enemy, but as a person who denied himself the opportunity to feel the love I had for him.

This exercise can be done with any past negative relationship, even after the person has passed on. We must find ways to deal with it or it haunts us. We can save ourselves by changing our vocabulary.

Years later, there was still some level of discontent when thinking about my childhood and the disparity, leaving me in a negative frame of mind. I learned more about *his* early

childhood trauma. I had an intense hypnotherapy session
with the transformation coach, Jeff Faldalen, to help me
finally dismiss any threads of anger and resentment
around this issue. The way he was, had nothing to do with
me. He did the best he could manage to do. Today, it is
almost impossible to think of my father without feeling
sorry for him.

I took bold action by getting hypnotized. It had to be
bold; we always have the payoff of people feeling sorry for
us when we have a sad story. It's enticing to enroll people
in our victim-self, to get the reaction we crave. This
attention keeps us stuck in victim mode.

However, being a victim comes with an incredibly and
dangerous high price. We make the choice: remain as
victim or take the steps to be fully invested in our future
without this quicksand drowning us.

Going from angry to empathetic and forgiving is healthy
for us, regardless of the person, the crime, the pain, the
history, or the need to be a victim. Interpersonal
relationships bring out the best and the worst in us. They
usually start out great, but as the layers start to peel back
and the true Self is exposed, people respond at more
primal levels. In close relationships, we look for people
who reflect the persona we want for ourselves. Through
their behavior, we see ourselves. There are theories that we
are always inviting people into our lives to resolve our

family of origin issues. When we are conscious to this behavior, it is easier to recognize.

Friendships

The friendships we choose support or sabotage our happiness, harmony, and growth. Much like the interpersonal relationships, our close friends are a center of influence and have a profound effect on our outcomes. When I give a lecture to students, I often use this slide of a pyramid like this...

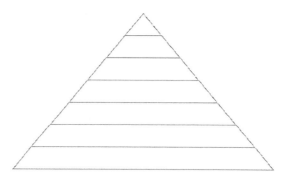

I like this visual, as it represents the levels of growth friends go through as one person is building and growing a future, while others are not. We're born into different levels on this pyramid, depending on our family's social standing. As we change, grow, and reach for our dreams, we move up a row at a time. With each level of growth, we become the reflection of inadequacy to the friends we leave behind.

For every friend who wants to attach their gravitational pull downward on us, we must find friends who want to pull us up to the next level, lifting as they climb, to where they operate.

When our centers of influence are stuck in miserable situations they tend to diminish our accomplishments as a way to appease their own anxiety or lack of ability to take action. Family members, co-workers, and peers, who don't truly support our growth, also do this. When we start to hear undermining comments from people who were previously positive (when we were thinking and behaving just like them), then we may need to consider allowing less influence from this person in our life. Moving on from a friendship does not mean we like this person less. It means our thinking and desires no longer align with theirs. Not any better, not any worse, just different. It's not healthy to suppress ourselves, to keep unsupportive friends around.

When this happens, hold dear to the positive memories, the history and the bonds we shared. Reframing the scope of any relationship is acceptable as long as we don't hurt anyone with our words or actions. Being graceful as we grow is never regrettable.

Friendships rich in trust, laughter, and support, are treasures. Making time for them is necessary!

Professional Relationships

Co-workers are like having a second family. We leave these people at the end of each day. The next day we wake up and see them again. If our intention is building a long term business that grows year after year, we need the right people. In this section, I'd like to give you some tools and processes for hiring the right people, attracting the best clients, and dealing with conflict if/when it arises.

Attracting Ideal Clients

All money is not created equal. The difference between our clients and any other relationship is we're receiving money for providing services. We're expected to behave as an elevated professional. As a result, we treat this relationship with specific care.

Some clients drain our energy, cost us money, and intentionally sabotage our good name, when they perceive our value as lesser than they expected. Others fill our heart with so much gratitude, pay us well, and rave for the rest of their lives. It's critically important to attract the right clients while repelling the mismatches.

Ideally, we want to attract clients who:

- Value our service and skills.
- Appreciate our advice and suggestions.
- Pay us on time.
- Refer us to their friends and colleagues.

- Are pleasant.
- Are energizing to work with.

When we are in our groove at work, our clients feel it. If we want the benchmark of how we come across to our clients, look at how they come across to us. Clients reflect our energy. We have the ability to lead them up or down.

We don't realize how much power we have over clients, so it never occurs to us to use it ethically. They are attracted to us because they want what we have, literally. If we stop here, we have successfully figured it out.

But, we pander, because they pay us.

When we take control of a client situation, delivering more than expected, outperforming our competitors, and adding value wherever we can, we win them for life. This is in *our* hands!

When we lose a client to a competitor, one of three things has happened: they found someone who offered a newer idea or product; they found someone who they perceived to be better, or better value; they found someone who offers something totally different than we do.

Taking a client for granted, will drive them out the door. They can sense the very second this happens. Getting left in the dust is hard to swallow.

In the *Grow Your Business* chapter, I'll be covering more in-depth tactics to choose your ideal clients.

The Love/Hate Relationship
between Employers and Employees

Since the beginning of time, there has been a gap in what both the employer and employee believe about each other. We never speak of it, but I believe it is the underlying cause of every issue in the employment realm.

I generalize here. But for sake of improvement, please assume this may be happening in your company.

As employers, we yearn to surround ourselves with people we trust. We count on our co-workers to represent our name. We need them to protect our vision, our products, our services, and ensure those products and services get delivered to our clients and customers. To get this result, we work at these relationships by design, not by default. Our relationship with clients or co-workers in many regards, are the same. They take thought and effort. It's always easier to figure it out with people we are not sleeping or sharing holiday meals with.

We tend to replicate the past with the primary people in our companies. We hire 'the daughter we wish we had', 'he's like the brother we loved', or 'the sister who was so much fun'. Look closely....You can usually see the threads of similarity.

For those of us lucky enough to employ people long term, we've had to learn how to do a dance with our staff. While we lead, we take their cues on which moves to make next. It is gentle. It is thoughtful. It is responsible. This is not a class we take for credits. This is an on-the-job skill that is learned, honed and perfected over the years. But be alert, we can only control ourselves and many people are masterful at disguising their agendas.

I bought my first business, a hair salon, when I was nineteen. Putting myself through college, I left after one semester, with no formal business training. Until that point, I had been interviewed for jobs in high school, but I hadn't conducted an interview to hire an employee. I learned how to hire by asking my clients, while they sat in the chair during their haircut. I kid you not; this was the only resource I had at the time. There were no support systems for young females in business like myself, who didn't have a formal education. Business books were far and few between. Honestly, I felt intimidated about the whole situation. I did whatever I could to scrape together enough money to buy the business and pay the rent.

The beauty of going into a business at a young age is that I was so naïve. I had no clue what I didn't know. The only thing I was certain of is that I would figure it out. Maybe clumsily and disjointed I had no choice but to succeed.

Losing my first salon in a tragic fire, I had to rebuild. This was harder than I can explain here, but to say I put my heart and soul into reinventing my lost business is an understatement. When I reopened several months later, my new business was better in every way. It provided room for growth of additional services and expanded staff.

After putting 100% of my trust into people I hired, many times, I got burned. They became my friends. Then it got harder to reprimand them when they were breaking policies and hurting my business. Very early on, one of the employees I trusted most showed me I needed to learn more about making better hires. I will refer to her as Jane.

Jane worked with me at the first location, stayed on into the second location and stayed as I was preparing to open another salon in an up and coming area of the city. This newest location would include Day Spa services, which were mostly unheard of at the time. Jane was my daily confidante. It was a hectic time. My first child was only a few weeks old when I decided he deserved a better life than the one we could currently offer him.

As I placed my attention and energy on making plans for the new location, nursing an infant, and working behind the styling chair five days a week, I was not aware of the shift in Jane's personality.

My lease was nearing its end. I previously approached Jane about purchasing the business so I could fully focus on the new location. We negotiated a fair price and good terms with a decent timeline. I needed the funds to pay off a short term loan I had borrowed for the new equipment I was purchasing. We announced it to our clients, who were planning a surprise party for Jane. It all seemed like a great plan.

A few days before the final papers and money were to be exchanged, the landlord called me. My employee circumvented me. Jane went directly to the landlord and said she would not be purchasing my business, since I was already moving, she would take over the lease when it lapsed. She would then make me an offer on the inventory and equipment. I was floored. I loved Jane! Knowing I had to fire her immediately, I was a wreck. I laid awake most of the night playing it out. My husband had a solid career, but without the business proceeds, we could not afford the loan payments. I went to the salon before sunrise, packed up her belongings and sat waiting. When she arrived, I thanked her for her few years of service and let her go. When she asked me why, I explained I was aware of her deception, and although she was a great employee, the business I had built was not hers for the taking. I handed Jane her box of belongings and asked her to leave.

To this point, this was the hardest thing I had to do with an employee. I share this story because if you have not encountered a similar situation, you almost certainly will. Regardless of the annual revenue in your company, there is almost always someone lurking, believing they deserve what you have built. Some act on it, some don't.

In my case, those types of scenarios happened when I let an employee get too close to me, or if I cared more about their happiness instead of my own. When we turn work relationships into personal relationships, things change. Our fears, attachments, and vulnerability, cause us to miss important cues about people. It's easy to ignore these feelings, continuing to compromise our boundaries. This happens to owners of small businesses run from basements, up to CEO's of major corporations.

The episode with Jane led me to change my interviewing process. There was incongruence between my values and some of my hires. I started looking for common values before I looked for experience. Once I gleaned this information during the interview, I could better know if the potential employee would be more in line with my style of communication, priorities, and expectations.

When entering into *any* relationship, core values count, both personally and professionally. Aligning ourselves with people who are vastly different than we are sets the stage for chaos.

We attract the right employees into our business if we consider a few key elements about their personality. Pay attention when you're unnecessarily making compromises to appease an employee - this is a red flag. There are some questions that can help reestablish new boundaries with existing employees. Please consider the following:

- Is your interview process thoroughly designed to save headaches in the future?
- Does your training process include clear expectations and outcomes?
- Are you holding all employees to the same standard?
- Are you as professional as you need to be?
- Is your communication clear and concise?
- Do you hold people accountable?
- Are you comfortable firing people when necessary?
- Are you clear on the core values you're looking for?

What if we hire an employee and they turn out to be a wrong fit? Usually people weed themselves out. They start to get themselves in trouble, which is their issue, not ours. They can wreak havoc in the system if not kept in check. If we believe in the person, and have empathy and skills to help them, we can sometimes turn them around. However, it's not easy. Some people have programmed themselves to believe they are not worthy of having a great job, or we represent something to them that reminds them (at a subconscious level) of what they need to work out with authority figures. But hang in there. If our intention comes from an authentic place of wanting them to grow, even if it means leaving us to start their own business, then it's worth the time we put in. I caution: sometimes people are looking for therapists when we are nice to them. Be kind, be gentle, know your limitations and draw the line when needed.

With a manipulative personality, you need to quickly deal with or remove them. Otherwise, you'll end up paying a high price. Manipulators can take a thread of truth and twist it around to get the results they want. He or she has usually developed this skill over time. Sometimes you see it and sometimes you don't. When things aren't adding up, there's a reason and a person behind the curtain calling the plays. Manipulators stir the pot. Then, they walk away innocently, as they laugh up their sleeve.

When we've grown up with manipulators, we need to be cautious. We tend to attract them in various shapes and sizes, into our business and our personal life. If you find *yourself* rewording the account of what actually happened, you could question yourself on why this behavior is comfortable. What rewards do *you* get for manipulating? How much energy do you spend convincing people *your* story is true?

Humans are survivors. We have learned many forms of how to look like the winner. Winning, at another's expense, eventually undermines our own confidence. Think of times you've done this in some form, every human being has. No one is above making wrong judgement calls or big mistakes. We can only fix it, apologize, learn from it, and move on. If we owe an apology, clean it up with the other party. Going back to apologize for a miscommunication which happened years ago frees your mind to move forward without a tiny anchor of bad juju.

If you have erred and attempt to clean it up, expect one of three possible outcomes: the other party has no recollection of the event; the other party accepts your apology and you both move on; the other party refuses to accept your apology and has since reinvented the story to tilt their way. If this happens, they can never forgive you. They simply do not know how.

Managing Volunteers

Paid employees have an obligation to respond to us. Volunteers are a different story. People step up because of their passion around an area, usually related to something personal in their history that drives them to help. Because they volunteer precious time and money, they may feel entitled to do their own thing. Volunteers need to be thanked by their leaders for everything. They also need to be corrected when their behavior negatively affects the cause.

During the years I chaired the Board of Governors for a Domestic Violence Shelter, a most uncomfortable situation occurred, when I had to censure a dear friend who was serving alongside me. Her heart was absolutely in the right place, but the counselors felt micromanaged.

We had to keep a level of consistency for kids in the shelter, regarding daily routines, food choices, and family support. The experienced and certified staff knew what worked. When kids are moved emergently to temporary housing, they need to be handled like fragile little rose petals. Some of my friend's behavior was disrupting the staff routine and harmony. I should have stepped in a few months earlier, but this was a volunteer job for me too. I was already consumed with chairing a board of directors without personal issues adding to my responsibilities. My friend was a dedicated, sweet, wonderful woman, who was simply not seeing how her attention to detail affected others. I sought counsel on the issue, and with the presence of the gentlest soul on the board, we three discussed the issues. It was not a banner day, by anyone's account.

It took years for us to repair our friendship. The lesson I learned, was to nip situations in the bud before they grew into big weeds. This is true in every area of life.

Leadership is not for the fragile soul. Tough decisions take a toll on us. As an elected leader, our priority is governing for an overarching benefit. Personal feelings get cast aside as the organization we have been entrusted with, is counting on our strengths. People elect us because they want results. They do not care deeply about our personal life or unexpected interruptions. If they did, we would not be running the meetings.

When I look back at this opportunity to serve my community, it is clear the Board Chair needed to be tough, passionate, and unyielding to external or personal discomfort. It's not easy to shift a community's thinking about taboo subjects happening in their backyard. When I was anxious about uncomfortable situations dealing with board members or volunteers, I only had to see the face of a battered woman or child in the shelter to get over myself.

People find each other and their voices when they need to. Nothing is by coincidence. Every single event that happens in our life is the result of a decision we make. If we are broadsided in our car, with no responsibility for a drunk driver who did this to us, we are still responsible for putting ourselves in our car at that time and that place. Blaming others for what happens in our life, keeps us weak and disempowered.

Taking responsibility for our current circumstances, our company, our organization, or the Boards we lead, is the key to making positive changes.

Conflict Resolution

Conflict arises when a person feels fear, which leads to frustration, which leads to acting out, which leads to staffing issues and revenue losses. Remembering that fear is the driving force, allows us to approach conflict from a higher perspective point.

Conflict manifests in two common ways: first, the staff member isolates themselves, starts acting like a jerk, loses respect, loses connections at work, jeopardizes our clients, and then, eventually they're gone. Usually an outside source who is hearing a one-slanted side of the story, is giving this person advice.

When this happens, we hear comments like "What was going on with him?", "I saw this coming for months," "She was more focused on taking her kids' calls than she was on our clients' needs." Human behavior is fascinating. It is similar across all levels of income, status, and education.

The other manifestation is when the employee is covert, stays with us, and wreaks some level of havoc in our organization. One of the biggest challenges in management communication is a term called "Triangulation." I've watched it happen for decades. Here's an example: persons A and B have a disagreement. Person A comes to us with their story, explaining how person B is wrong. Person B goes to a co-worker with their story, of how person A is wrong. They're both building their camps of support. Before we know it, there is unrest, undermining, and mistrust in our organization.

No matter who we work with, we need to communicate needs and set boundaries. It's a two-way street. Encourage and help co-workers to set their boundaries as well. My spa director, Jonelle, is one of the best at getting people back in their own lanes. She does it with grace and ease, with a smooth outcome guaranteed. By using her unique skills, she deflects many conflicts. This shields me, the staff, and the clients from disruption.

There are a few ways to handle disruptive conflict. It's best to never meet alone with a staff member when there is an issue. Bring in a neutral person such as H.R., department manager, or lawyer if it is serious, but don't meet without a witness to the conversation. If you're recording a meeting for learning or factual purposes, all parties must agree in writing, for it to be recorded.

Bringing both people/sides together, by mediating in a way where each person knows we have heard and understood their position, because we have repeated it back to them, is a great way to build trust among staff.

Once we understand where pain and frustration comes from, it's easier to work through it with others. We can never get this clear information from hearsay. It must come first hand from the involved parties.

If both parties agree to a group meeting, describe what each side is thinking and feeling, then announce the desired outcome of the mediation, in a way that leaves everyone wanting to end on common ground.

It's important to lay out a clear set of ground rules for this type of situation. Write the terms on paper if you must. Use a timer. If tears start, ask the crying one to step out and compose themselves. Tears are typically how they get away with their antics. Don't fall for it.

If this seems like 'babysitting' which I hear from CEO's of Fortune 2000 companies to corner convenience store owners, it is important not to buy in to that feeling. When we approach our staff like they are babies, we send the message we are better and smarter than they are. They sense the subtle condescendence we feel. This leads to resentments which we will never hear spoken, because it happens at a subconscious level.

When people get defensive, they often go into a "child-like state" and view us as if we are their parent. Keeping this defensive mechanism in mind will help you maintain an objective outlook on reality. Their upset likely has nothing to do with you. It's also important to understand how easy it is to react to them, mimic their behavior, and start acting like a scolding parent figure. Do your best to avoid that trap.

For staff to see us concerned and curious, keeps us human. For staff to see us lose our temper, slam things, turn red in the face, blow steam, or f-bomb our head off, is an immediate recipe for loss of respect.

Outrageous displays can make us feel like we got their attention. Trust me, they all go home and talk about it over dinner. These negative stories about your temper are never what you want the conversation to be about.

People bring their baggage to work. Our job as the leader of the team is to help them rise above it. Creating a culture of positive and productive relationships within our organization is a constant priority for the owner and managers.

Culture is everything. Without it, sales don't happen. Service doesn't happen. Revenue doesn't happen. Strong reputation doesn't happen. Speaking to people in a direct and truthful way, filled with appropriate levels of emotion, always gets results. Faking any of the above, will come back to haunt us. If not immediately, we will see numbers and people fall away. I've been involved with organizations where this happens. If I'm not in a position to fix a bad situation, I responsibly resign.

Lead the way to the best staff possible. Clients, employees, siblings, best friends, partners, and children, cannot think or feel like we do. Expecting this is sheer lunacy. Getting people to see and feel our *vision,* takes creativity in our delivery. Having our team live up to their highest level of performance, should always be our primary goal. This translates into higher satisfaction and sales.

When I was still interviewing people, I would expect they would be as good as their pitch. We need to be careful when we expect interview day enthusiasm to be present every day. It's unrealistic on our part.

It is realistic to spend our time focusing on setting relationship, performance, behavior, and monetary goals, as well as establishing crystal clear expectations and avenues for communication.

Just because we're super high producers, doesn't mean others are. If we dishonor staff by imposing unrealistic expectations, they become unmotivated and distrusting. During rapid growth mode, this turns out to be a roadblock that slows us down.

When opening my third Spa location in a ski resort, I experienced this. I'd put my kids to bed, and then work on my task list. I would prepare to-do lists for people on my management team.

Because they wanted to please me, they would nod in agreement. I took it at face value. When 14/20 items got done, I'd question what went wrong. I didn't stop to think about how much time away from their regular duties it took to accomplish my requests.

Being keenly sensitive to body language and facial expression while communicating, shows us what to do next. The more of the five senses used, the better our understanding. Emails and texts lack the intonation and feeling needed to convey and gather important information.

It was only through my intentional guidance of conversations, acknowledging my mistakes at the outset, where I could learn what staff needed and how I was going about things the wrong way.

An example: with my hand gently on her shoulder (this is the spa industry, we accept respectful touch) "Candice, I know how difficult your primary role is, and I realize I've burdened you with my daily task lists to help get the new location up and running." Candice then could honestly respond, because I gave her permission to speak to my fault. "Yes, Dorothy, it really is a full-time and full energy job to manage the daily operation here. I'm falling short in all areas. I know you see this. Can anyone else take some of the tasks off my plate?" Eureka!!! The problem now had a solution.

By my giving Candice room to speak openly, she was able to help me see where she needed support and I was expecting too much. We adjusted and moved on. Shoulders dropped, the pressure valve was released when I recognized I controlled it. Her husband thanked me the next time he saw me.

Our staff always talks about us at home. It is part of the gap we are blind and/or indifferent to as employers.

We changed the title of our group management meetings to "Journey of Success". I still refer back to these meeting minutes, many years later, to remind myself when I feel I'm getting pushy.

Progress is important, focusing on perfection yields frustration. Meet people where they are. In every interaction, ask yourself, "How can I help this person feel important, respected, and honored – while honoring and respecting myself and my needs?"

When we put time and effort into creating the culture we want, it is incredibly rewarding. Be prepared, every single person who joins or leaves an organization, changes the culture within.

When we bring a new person on board, it's critical to have a training mechanism in place to make them feel comfortable, make them feel confident, and make them understand the importance of their participation in our culture.

When people don't know what to do or how to act within an organization, they make things up. When we're bringing someone new in, our existing staff should know and understand some things about this person. Do they have special needs? Have they joined our company as an award-winning salesperson? Are they an avid fisherman or hunter? Do they restore vintage cars? Is this their first role in a company like ours, where they need additional training?

Help your staff to form opinions of new employees by directing their focus on the information that is important to you. This makes the on-boarding process more seamless.

Sharing accolades and rewards with staff, will keep them with us longer. Acknowledgement for a good job is critical for every relationship, regardless of the category. The employee/employer relationship is the key to growing any company. Regardless, if we have one person, a leadership team, or several employees who rely on our daily input and guidance, our primary role is to make people happy so they chose to work with our company.

When staff situations feel overwhelming, it is perfectly acceptable to close your eyes, take a few deep breaths, and mentally go to your happy place!

MASTERING YOUR SPIRITUALITY

Don't get nervous. I'm not recruiting you into a religion. We're also not going to light incense or, "ohm," I promise. However, it's my contention that "faith in something bigger than us," is useful for living a successful life. I've found there are two types of faith. The first is faith in a higher *power* (God, Ala, the Universe, whichever term you use). The second type of faith is focused on a higher *purpose* (succeeding for something other than your personal desires). Either will improve your life. I've found that a combination of both is the best.

We need to recognize we're not the cause and effect of everything in our lives. This kind of thinking keeps us from being humble in good times and motivated in hard times.

Higher purpose and faith keeps us in check when things are "Explosively Great!" It could be that we're promoting a new product line or piece of equipment. We know there's competition from every other company in town. We sell out by the end of the first week. It's the best feeling. It could be that we're exceeding budget on a promo we didn't think would perform. Maybe we hired the ideal person who understands our vision; they treat clients with care and they're easy to work with.

When things are going well, we may think, "I am special. I did this all myself!" Do we also take full credit when things go south? When we're winning, it's time for giving thanks. It's time to reflect. It's time to keep our ego in check. That's how "higher purpose" keeps us humble in good times.

Running a great company is reason to celebrate ourselves, and we should. When it crosses the line to an ego driven situation, remembering there is something bigger than us, is what keeps us real.

Adversity is certain. We all have days that are "Explosively Awful!" It's that day as a restaurant owner when you get a recall on Romaine lettuce. When you're worried about a client eating something tainted. If they get sick or worse *die*, you are responsible. Maybe you accepted a large payment in the form of a personal check and it bounces. Perhaps you're pulling our hair out because you don't have enough money to cover payroll. A client got a chemical burn, or a passerby had a slip and fall on our sidewalk during a snowstorm. Our largest client's 90-day payment terms are stretched to 120 days, and our line of credit isn't large enough. Bad reviews. Negative press. Floods. Fires.

In whatever way negative situations appear in our business, faith in a higher power or purpose will pull us through. Faith provides the extra fuel when we hit empty.

Feeling isolated, is a natural part of being an entrepreneur. Yet, as a leader, we cannot allow ourself to transfer those feelings to our clients, customers, fans, and employees. In low moments, having faith in a higher power, helps ease those tensions and prevents them from affecting the people around us.

Belief systems are often passed down generationally. We believe what we learned as we were being raised. Generational religious beliefs can be rewarding and wonderful, unless those beliefs don't support who we are.

If you live an alternative lifestyle, some religions will not accept you with the love you deserve. Find a new path if you need to. I'm not telling anyone what to do. I'm simply saying, in my opinion, we need to believe there is a force above ourselves.

Deeply *faithful* people, in my experience, accept others, respect others, and want to help others. They are genuine. I've also witnessed people who claim to be deeply *religious,* who perform unkind acts, deception, and harmful deeds. They wave the flag of religion, as if this public demonstration neutralizes their inner demons. Loud and public religious rants are sometimes designed to take the spotlight off deeply private guilt, beliefs, and actions.

Shame over inner beliefs causes humans to create a great act to cover things up. In the movie *The Reader,* the main character, portrayed by Kate Winslett, committed suicide, so her secret would never be exposed. Based on a true story, she never learned how to read. Making it through life pretending to be something we are not leads to guilt, illness, anger, and mistreatment of anyone who gets close to what we are hiding.

One of the hardest things we can do is to accept *our truth* and express it without apology. The shame we feel, keeps us from living our best authentic life. If we've buried our sexual fantasies because we're ashamed of them, our partners will never satisfy us. We build our daily life around protecting our innermost secrets. Usually, people care far less about our inner secrets than we ever expect. We ruminate, build a story in our heads, and then live our life as if this story is true.

Guilt forces us to overcompensate in other ways, which then builds resentment. We prevent ourselves from showing who we really are for fear of rejection. This ruins many relationships.

Religious guilt, once a standard, has turned many people away from church, when they believe it's used as a control mechanism.

Faith in a force greater than us keeps the significance of our own imperfection in balance. This can help when we're being true to ourselves and living unencumbered by a need to keep secrets. We can remain humble in good times and overcome internal barriers more easily in hard times.

Adherents.com is an independent, non-religiously affiliated organization that offers statistics about different religions worldwide. According to their citations, there are over 4,200 different religions. If you're looking for a spiritual framework to follow, there is an abundance to choose from.

Religion and Faith are distinctly different from each other. They are deeply personal and individual decisions.

I changed from believing I would be a Catholic Nun, spending time in the summers at a Convent in upstate New York, to questioning some teachings of the Bible. I searched for a few years to find what I was looking for. I had faith in God, but didn't want the guilt that came along with being a Catholic. I found my place in the Lutheran Church, with a Pastor whom I deeply respected, for his neutral position and non-judgement of individuals and circumstances. I may change again in the future, but I'm very clear I will always look to a higher power than myself, whatever denomination I choose to find it in.

I abandoned the convent because I no longer shared the idea women are inherently wrong. I asked, "Why is Eve blamed for Adam biting the apple?"

The Higher Purpose Approach

Regardless of our feelings on a religious power, creating a higher purpose shifts the importance of everything in life.

A higher purpose is what we hold in the highest regard of importance. Operating our life, our company, and our financial responsibilities within this framework, shifts stress and shutdown into opportunity and appreciation. When we create a huge purpose that is not about our own personal wealth, it changes how we approach everything.

Several years ago my mother had a stroke. She wasn't expected to live, but she did. The stroke happened on the

Saturday before Easter in 1998. After weeks in the hospital, my mom regained some speech and very little strength. Upon release, she stayed with my sister for six weeks, but it was too difficult with the many stairs in her house.

I brought mom to live with me and my sons. My new company was only a few months old, giving chaos a new meaning. I was working seven days a week to get things organized. I was by now single with six and ten year old sons, in the middle of moving into a new house, and getting my kids registered into the new school system, where they would be starting the following week. My life was filled with pressure. The daily nursing help I hired was not enough. By December, I realized my mom needed more care than we could give her. We found a wonderful personal care home, and placed her there in a private room. I believed she had enough funds to cover about five years of expenses, if she lived that long. She was happy when she had lucid moments. I felt a great sense of relief, knowing she was being cared for at an optimal level.

Several months later, I went to Europe for a few weeks to look at new product lines. When I returned, my mother had been moved to a much lesser facility, where she now shared a room with three other women. She was not getting bathed. I couldn't get straight answers from my siblings about my mother's finances. I learned the checks had been bouncing and my mother was asked to leave the first facility. I didn't have power of attorney for my mother, so I was unable to access her accounts to find the problem. I went to speak to the family friend who managed her bank accounts. I learned there truly was no money left in any of her accounts, including one she shared with me. Every penny with her name on it was gone. I was furious and scared. I had no support in the situation. My oldest brother had passed years earlier. He would never have allowed this situation to occur. I missed him and his wisdom. I had to figure it out on my own.

As upset as I was, I needed to get my mother to a better place before anything else. I left the bank, went back to the nursing home, and asked if I paid the rent in advance, giving my personal oath that I would never be late with a payment, would they consider taking my mother back. They agreed and I moved her back the next day.

Upon return from the move, I sat at my desk and thought about my mother's needs. She was becoming my single largest expense. A light bulb in my mind turned on. I looked back at what I had accomplished in the past twenty years. I knew I had the skills, smarts, and strength to do this. I had just been caught up in day-to-day operations of what was now a spa with two locations. My fear was replaced by fierce determination to take care of my helpless mom.

Utilizing my mother's needs as the higher purpose for my company's success, allowed me to take the focus off myself, my stress, and the belief I had to do everything. It was the motivation to systematize and delegate better. We developed a Policy and Procedure guide, which provided staff with clear answers in every category. I took myself out of operations, and focused solely on the growth aspect of the company. Over the next four and half years of my mother's life, I more than doubled our annual revenue, opened a third spa location, started a separate boutique Bed and Breakfast business, paid off debt, bought a second home in a ski resort area located on a pristine lake, and provided my sons with a future that looked very different than the year before my mother's stroke.

When my mother passed, I had the gratifying knowledge that her expenses were funded by the business that held her as its higher purpose. I expected to cry at her funeral and deeply grieve her loss. Instead, I realized our relationship was completed in every possible way. There was nothing left I wished I would have said, or could have done for her. The lesson learned from losing my father before we got it all on the table, taught me to finish all business and conversations with people I love, because we never know when our turn is up.

Seeing the benefits of operating for a cause more meaningful than my own, helped me make a decision. We vowed to donate 10% of our gross revenue to charities our team is passionate about. During the years of the recession, this was tough. I missed months of income to keep my promise. I simply forced myself to be better in business. Had I not set up my life in a way where I could do this, it would not have worked out. As our revenue grew, I always held the fear that it could stop at any time. Paying off debt was the positive byproduct of having positive revenue. By removing the pressure of personal debt, my mind was even clearer to focus on the needs of my children and my company.

If you're not sure what to passionately embrace, volunteer within your local community to learn what strikes a chord.

As I referenced above, I served for six years on the board of a Domestic Violence shelter. From 2007 through 2010, I chaired the Dove Center Domestic Violence and Sexual Assault Resource Center. This is a local shelter building where a mother and her children could go to if; for instance, her spouse became violent at home. She and her kids could receive counseling and support at the center, as well as hotline services, school outreach, and future support programs.

This type of work is important to me because I have experienced domestic violence in a relationship firsthand.

Taking a stand for women is important to my soul's evolution.

Being one of the rare females to have the honor of chairing this board, I needed to be exemplary in my words and actions. I sought advice from my Pastor, Rev. Dr. Scott Robinson, as a mentee on conducting Robert's Rules of Order. We were in a Capital Campaign, driving hard to get a new shelter we desperately needed. We lost the first round and the board was deflated. I came back to our next meeting with energy and strategy to motivate them. The board bought in. Members, feeling we really could win the grant money if we raised enough locally, started fundraising events that are now annual events for the community. Once we realigned on the effort, we raised the funds to get the match from the state. Our new shelter was built in 2011 with money raised by fabulous people and generous donors, on ideal property that was partially donated by a local surgeon.

How did we do this? Domestic violence is a taboo subject in any community. In order for people to donate, they had to first be comfortable saying the words, "Domestic violence is a problem in our community." Then they had to feel a sense of ownership over the shelter, as if it were theirs, which of course it would be, as it was built with their money.

The Executive Director, Heather, and I, went right into the middle of local meetings. It was easy for me to talk about the impact, the incessancy, and the generational patterns, moving my words into the hearts and emotions of the people in the audience. Heather talked about the specifics of the organization, the funding, the clients, the state of the overcrowded current shelter, and programs for abusers.

Between my mother's situation, chairing the board of the D.V. center, and then later chairing a capital campaign with my husband, Daryl, to build a cancer care center in the rural community where we lived, I felt a great sense of higher purpose; a purpose which was independent from my faith. Yet, the underlying feeling was similar. When things in my business were running smoothly, my mother and the women at the shelter kept me humble. When business was becoming hard, their reminder kept my chin up.

Having a higher purpose in life and in business can change our world. Not having a higher purpose can leave us with nothing more than possessions that one day, become our ball and chain. Giving attention to our faith and purpose every day, can serve as a moral compass at any time of life.

MASTERING YOUR CAREER AND EDUCATION

How many people do you know who go through life miserable due to their job? Also, how many people do you know who deservedly earned a reputation for something work related, only to fall from grace when the business cycle changed and their relevance was less important? And how many people do you know who have never felt like they worked a day in their life, yet they put in tremendous hours and produced tremendous results?

We spend most of our waking hours earning wages to provide food and shelter for our families. If that time isn't enjoyable, we set ourselves up for illness, headaches, fatigue, and failure in other areas. I've watched individuals wreck great relationships, allowing misguided negativity and blame to be in the wrong place.

Career discontent, occurs when we're afraid to make the changes we need, when we stop learning and growing, and when we shortchange our worth by performing at a lower level, knowing we are more capable.

When we stay in an unfulfilling job or career, solely for the money, we are prostituting ourselves for a paycheck.

When I look at masters of communication, famous people such as Mary Kay Ash, Joel Bauer, Tony Robbins, Stephen Covey, or Jack Canfield, I wonder what keeps them going. I can only assume since they deal in human growth based on personal insights, that their fuel is the reward of watching their mentees go into the world and make a difference.

Witnessing the growth of an individual, a process, a product, or a company, knowing we are an integral part of this growth, is one of the most rewarding things we can partake in.

When we face career challenges, we are forced to make decisions we have not planned for. How flexible we are, determines how successfully we respond to those incoming missiles.

In the 1990's, I had just been elected to preside over an international organization in the beauty industry. I was thirty-five years old at the time. I was the first female and the youngest person to hold such a position. My first official duty was to meet a group of Japanese delegates in New York to discuss details of an international educational event, taking place six months later. I was nervous and not sure I knew what to do, or how to do it. There was no guide. The outgoing President, Tony Fanelli, a thoughtful, generous, and wonderful man, was very helpful. But his experience was from a single and male perspective. I was married with young children.

The day I was flying home from New York, my house caught on fire due to an electrical storm. My mother and

Julian, four at the time, were in the house. They didn't suffer any harm, but we lost all of our possessions.

While I was arranging temporary housing, buying clothes, toothbrushes, and daily necessities, a key employee was caught skimming cash. I had to let her go. Not only this, I learned my bank accounts were jeopardized.

The regional director of the organization called to ask if I needed to step down to handle my multiple personal crises. This ran in the same vein as my father telling me I wasn't smart enough and he'd watch me fail when I was buying a business at the age of nineteen. The very thought that I was incapable, compelled me to work harder.

I had to take on the task of forensically detailing my books. Computer software was new at this time, and none of us knew how to use it. So, I did everything by hand and long math. This was while simultaneously running my business, managing a full staff, generating revenue, presiding over an international organization, and raising children.

By this time, my marriage had been faltering for a few years. We made a private decision to stay together until my term would be up, to keep our kids more secure in one home. As I mentioned, an agreeable separation, by intention, eliminates personal chaos beyond compare.

Entering detailed bookwork was not my strong suit. Finding missing money from bank accounts was not either. I was devastated and self-doubting when I learned what happened. I needed loyalty and support during this time, not sharks in the water. These few months were a very difficult phase of life. In the end, a client who specialized in business law, advised me to let it go. The money, we calculated to be near $50,000, was long gone.

Sometimes you have to cut your losses and move forward regardless of your pride. Producing higher revenues, focusing on the future, and securing our assets is better than attempting to fight for a lost cause. When self-serving individuals have more available time than we do, then they have more time to fight us. Move on.

When things are going well in a career, it's easy to get caught up in the applause. Be intent to keep growing, learning, teaching, and contributing, more importantly than accepting accolades.

Stay humble and strive for bigger opportunities. If we're not growing and innovating, we're becoming obsolete. Look at Blackberry. They owned the business oriented handheld device market. Today, if you're under twenty-five, you likely have no idea what a Blackberry was.

When we become fixated on one specific product or area of our career, we become dangerously close to becoming uni-dimensional and being known for 'having a mullet'.

Remember the mullet? How many individuals do we know who are stuck in a time warp with their hair, makeup, fashions, and beliefs? The growth stopped at the point they viewed it to be their pinnacle of success.

Y2K is a great example. People built careers on the premise that the world would come to a screeching stop on midnight of January 1, 2000. Then it was 12:01 and we all had running water. The need to learn something new, make progress, and proceed, is what keeps our confidence up. We wither when we stop learning and growing. Being a hard-boiled individual and not taking help or direction from others when we need it, turns us into bland and boring people.

When I mentor entrepreneurs one-one-one, the question always arises, "How do I know what kind of business to open?" My response is to find the thing you love to do the most in your life, and figure out how to turn it into a business.

When we earn our living working in an area we love, it never feels like work. Every friend who owns or manages a sports gear store, manages a health club, or teaches people how to golf, is doing what they love to do. On their free time, they bike, swim, and golf. In their mind, they're playing. They're getting paid for doing what they would be doing regardless. They have bridged the gap from having fun alone, to sharing fun at a professional level. They use their own expectation of what is great customer service, great equipment, and a great culture, as a benchmark, for what they provide.

We also tend to build businesses that solve a dilemma from our childhood. My friends who felt insecure as children due to unstable family situations, own security businesses and protective services.

Many people in the beauty profession have an innate need to help others feel beautiful, as their way to feel more attractive themselves. Chefs often grow up with a need to eat better food. Engineers build strong foundations....you get the idea. In general, people find what inspires them when they allow themselves to think about it, without worrying they will disappoint their dad.

Once we find our ideal career, being the very best we can be, involves continued learning. Exposing ourselves on a regular basis to learning opportunities is critical to staying current and passionate.

Teaching what we know solidifies our confidence and attracts positive energy into our fields.

Learning new hobbies and skills outside of work is equally important, if we want to maintain a sense of personal joy. New skills build confidence, regardless of our age. When children see us stretch our goals, they believe they can too. When our staff sees us struggle with a new technology, it keeps us human. Asking for help and demonstrating a willingness to learn something that is challenging, is a great leadership quality.

I'm a believer that when we teach, we learn. When I want to take on something new, I learn what I can comprehend, then put myself in a position to teach it to others.

Recently my church congregation lost our youth leader. When this happened, I was the President of Church Council. I was going to church every week already, arriving one hour earlier, to teach the program would not be that hard. I purchased the books, and decided I would teach the best and most fun class these kids could get. For teenagers to get to church an hour earlier on Sundays, it needs to be worth it. Over the next four years, I watched this group of kids blossom as we learned and discussed together, what we believed were the most important pieces of our history.

Being authentically myself, demonstrating that we don't have all the answers, but we can seek them from people who are more knowledgeable than we are, in the generous spirit of camaraderie, was one of the best things I have done. Had I not pushed myself and instead slept in one more hour on Sunday mornings, allowing someone else to lead the youth program, I would have lost that rich opportunity.

We gain confidence when we help others improve. We enjoy career happiness when we feel the positive impact we have on other human beings and systems. Find the gaps where unrest lives. Figure out what you need to do. Only you can discover the answers for yourself.

To fix a bad situation, give yourself a timeline and specific goals. If you're not sure what to do or how to do it, find a coach or a program and enroll yourself. Your gut will tell you when you're on the right path. You'll feel it when you're energized and look forward to something. If you feel drained and dreading, then delegate the task to someone who is better at it than you are.

Admitting the truth about our career when we're unfulfilled leaves us feeling vulnerable. However, it's the only way to move forward. Hoping, thinking, and pretending only means that we are not in alignment with our capabilities.

Speak intentions into existence, and then follow up on them. Our *word* is the only thing that can never be taken away from us. Keep your word. If you're in over your head, discuss it, don't deny it. People see right through it sooner than later. We lose credibility when we quit what we promised we would finish.

Be true to yourself. You can never expect anyone else to provide you with the life you want. You are the key to the happiness in your career.

Feeling stagnant leads to boredom and this gets leaders into trouble. If I'm not busy enough with what I've got going on, I make up new stuff to do. Not everyone is like this. But if you're frustrated, challenge yourself. I've learned new skills, studied new languages and met fabulous people just by making up something new to do.

How do you know when it's time? It's usually when you're pestering people over pedestrian things.

When we set goals, we give ourselves something to measure our progress. I'm a list-maker. The act of crossing items off my list is totally empowering. It builds the feeling of confidence, capability, and self-esteem.

My lists usually contain three categories of tasks: easy, mid-range, and the dreaded thing I try to put off. Here is a truth: if we get the dreaded tasks over with first, our energy and confidence skyrocket. Often times, the other items fall off the list.

Meeting high goals is the intent, but not always necessary. It's the byproducts that happen along the way, where the differences in most of life and businesses are made. Often, halfway to a goal, it changes because we've learned something else. The goal needs to change, or we need a better opportunity. We can never receive this positive consequence, if we don't start with the intention to do something new, something better, and something different!

In 2003, I was in a Strategic Coach® workshop, based in Toronto. The founder, Dan Sullivan, is one of the most brilliant and practical minds when it comes to concepts that grow a business. One of our workshops was finding the bottlenecks in our company. At that time, my bottleneck was Gift Card sales at Christmas. Our buyers were almost entirely men. A consistent line of approximately fifteen men, waited to buy gift cards in the two weeks leading up to December 25th. I had to stop spa services and my technicians all became gift card processors! This was all before online buying was a thing. I envisioned my website able to produce live, bar-coded gift cards, which could be printed from the convenience of a personal computer during non-business hours if needed. That concept did not exist in the marketplace yet. I interviewed three technology companies who all told me that my idea was impossible. The fourth company, at the time, was designing Dell Computer Systems. They were based in Pittsburgh. They said the technology didn't exist yet, and to build it would cost me well over $100,000. I couldn't afford to spend this on my good idea, with no proof anyone would ever want to buy a gift card online. I found a group from Carnegie Mellon University, who had a start-up called Novaurora. They explained they could patch together existing technology to create a program very close to the one I envisioned. In the end, for a $20,000 budget, we built the first online gift card sales program in the beauty industry.

That December, all marketing and advertising drove people to our website. I removed our phone numbers. This was risky business in 2003. Phone numbers were all we had besides our web addresses. We closed the spa at 6:00 p.m. on Christmas Eve. By 6:00 a.m. on December 25th, over $21,000 in gift card sales were made online. I watched them coming in every two minutes. I'd hold my breath, wait, and voila! Another order popped up. I popped some champagne. It was a great day.

We put press releases out over the following months. The story was getting international attention. I formed a new company, SpaEdge Inc. The legal fees were high. This was new territory. Online sales were still skeptical. I had to hire one of the largest firms in the city to incorporate and protect my idea. Wells Fargo was holding our credit card deposits for six month increments because they viewed online sales as high risk.

Almost immediately after the stories were printed, we started getting calls from spas around the country. We could transform the spa industry with this idea that came from a workshop around bottlenecks.

If we can provide a solution, we can transform anybody and anything. Once I saw how successful my idea was in my own company, and saw the new clients I was servicing,

I pitched the idea to Spafinder. They thought I was crazy. With each attempt, I couldn't get past the level-two person on the phone. I believe they viewed me as a wacky spa owner. It took them years to add online sales to their own shopping cart. It's ok, I was paying attention to what I was doing. While I could not trademark the process, we did copyright it. It was a great run, and one of my best ideas to date.

The ISPA (International Spa Association) magazine, *Pulse*, featured a story on me, where I zealously described the details and success I was having with the program. A few years later, everyone was offering online gift cards. If I had not placed myself into a coaching program, believing I was worth the time and money, I would never have thought about that new opportunity that changed my industry. Education is a primary key to personal growth, success, and satisfaction.

Consider the following:

- Do you have complaints about your current job, career, or level of education?
- What do you see as the best way to initiate change?
- By embracing where you are right now, what do you realize about your capabilities?
- If you wish things were different, even slightly, what does this look like?

- Are you writing ideas down to gain clarity?
- Are you currently giving time and energy to something that drains you?
- Do you see opportunities where you could initiate a new idea?

Helping others is the *being* part of being human. Please list a few organizations you know could benefit by your sharing of a skill or talent. This can be short or long term: walking dogs at a shelter once a month, decorating a float in a parade, or reading to kids in a shelter on a Friday night. There is an abundance of people who need your help, and you have an abundance of skills. How can you help others in a way you feel is energizing, not draining? What skills do you have that you can share?

Now, get more specific! Where do you see problems, challenges, and pitfalls, in your business or job? Write them down.

- Next, and more importantly, what first steps can you take to turn those negatives into positive benefits or opportunities for growth?
- Lastly, who do you need to help yourself, and what do you need to learn, to start gaining your own traction?

Writing down our thoughts is the best way to gain clarity!

Many years ago, I bought a blank booklet to keep a list of "The Best Lessons I've Learned." Some items on that list are personal accomplishments; time-tested processes that worked then and will likely work again in the future.

However, most items made it to the list by being very expensive mistakes, where I lost traction and money because I didn't know what I didn't know. I'll share some of that list in the following chapters. Whether it's a success or failure, the important element is *progress*. Gains and losses all represent your commitment to play the game of life. If you're playing the game, you are winning.

MASTERING YOUR FINANCES

Like everything else we've discussed about being more effective and happier in life, finances and our relationship with them are generational. Welfare begets welfare. Success begets success. Hard workers produce hard workers. Savers produce savers, and spenders produce spenders. Of course, these general rules are meant to be broken. There are always exceptions. Yet, for the majority of people, this is accurate.

I earned my first money, when our next door neighbor asked my mother if I could come over and "set" her hair. My mother was a hairdresser. If I wanted to be around her, I had to busy myself in her basement salon. Wigs were in fashion in the late 1960's, so I had plenty of wigs to keep me busy, trying to master the skill of smoothing hair with rollers, clips, combs, and hairspray. Luckily for me, my mom allowed me to play beauty shop for real. These are among my happiest childhood memories. The clients took notice that as a young child, I had a skill. I was in second grade when Mrs. Simon paid me a quarter to set her hair once each week.

I saved my quarters. Then one day they were gone. Someone stole my quarters. No one got in trouble, except me, for complaining about it. I started subconsciously believing I'd work for other people's benefits instead of my own. As a result, I attracted some people who did exactly what I expected them to do. When a *taker* runs into a brick wall, they simply move on to the next person. Takers only stop by our depot, when our vibe lets them know our wallet is open for their visit.

Look for patterns in the problem relationships in your life. They all trace back to a decision we made. These folks channel chaos directly to us.

Overcoming self-limiting beliefs is hard work. We face the weakest parts of ourselves. We must see people we love as flawed. It is worth the work to understand how deeply these beliefs affect us.

Resetting Beliefs about Money

Much of the chaos around service-based businesses stems from how finances are managed. Our beliefs determine our behavior. Controlling the process is up to us. It needs to be very specific, and everyone who handles the revenue or expenses in the company, needs to clearly understand and abide by what we want. This is a no-give area. Problems with money occur when we turn a blind eye, have unrealistic expectations, aren't knowledgeable enough in this area, and allow the wrong people to manage this part of our business, or we have a pre-existing condition around our relationship with money.

If we've been given money our whole lives, we may have feelings of entitlement, and victimhood when the gravy train stops. The same goes when cash rolls in and we expect it will always be this way. When we hit a bump, we need to be prepared. Disciplined money management can make or break a business, especially during the start-up years.

Thieves also have a mindset. They feel entitled to what is not theirs. When people are good at lying, they're usually good at stealing. When we catch people in lies, examine all aspects of what they handle: accounts, clients, vendors, debits, and revenue. This mindset pops up everywhere. It's why banks make employees take two weeks off. Whenever a manager or key person is gone for two weeks, the inconsistencies present themselves. Start digging when the first thing doesn't add up. I promise you will find more than you want to.

People are often led to cash (service) businesses because they like to get away with things, like evading taxes. Stealing from the government is theft, and the IRS will always find you. Operating "under the table" means there is always a table top preventing growth. Getting away with evading taxes isn't worth the fear factor we hold deep inside ourselves. It's likely not worth the fancy and extravagant things we can buy. Run clean books.

There are many people who are excellent with finances. They grew up with a strong set of monetary values. These people are who you want as your money managers, life partners, friends, and co-workers.

Consider the following:

- Are there people in your organization whom you have a negative gut feeling about, regarding money-handling practices?

If possible, find out if others feel the same way. Set up systems where only one person could be responsible at a time. This is painstaking, but not as painful as learning your deposits are being shorted, or your products are being stolen.

- Do things always add up?

This can almost always be tracked back to a change that put a particular person closer to what is being stolen. We need to look for changes in patterns and responsibilities.

- Do you have enough protective measures in your organization?

Using security cameras, two-person cash counting between shifts, and simply paying better attention are all detriments to theft.

- Are you as well educated as you need to be regarding how to manage the finances in a growing organization?
- If you've been stolen from by an employee, the story spreads like wildfire. This is when everyone involved needs to know exactly what steps you've put in place to stop it.

This is what I've learned to be true: 25% of employees will never steal, 25% of employees are always looking for ways to steal, and 50% of employees are on the fence. If you've had a long-term staff, there's a better chance the thieves have all weeded themselves out. When you have a large staff in a quick moving cash business, your chances of theft of money and inventory increase.

The other truth; employees who have money issues cannot be trusted near *your* assets. Desperate people make desperate moves. Protect what you work for.

Credit Score and Credit Cards

Knowing your credit score is the same as knowing what your weight is. Unless you know these numbers, you cannot know if you need to go on a food or a financial diet. The most important factor in borrowing money, besides showing proof you can pay it back, is your credit score. If you like to hold on to money and are slow to pay your bills on time, it will cost you. If you need to purchase things to prove you're important, doing it while you carry a credit card balance is risky business. If you aren't paying off your credit card debt each month, or at least within three months' time, you're living beyond your means. You have to borrow money from the bank every month in the form of high interest, to cover the costs of what you've convinced yourself you cannot live without.

If you have credit card debt right now, think of three things you currently spend money on, that you could stop and your life would not be affected in a negative way.

How realistic is it to stop or slow the unnecessary spending in all areas of life? If we can't stop buying expensive coffee instead of making our own, then pick something else. If we struggle to pay bills, yet we enjoy eating dinner in a restaurant every day, perhaps we could strike a compromise with ourselves. The point is to know what your tolerance level is regarding what you can do without, to pay down debt and accumulate cash.

Stop voicing complaints about your financial situation if you haven't taken steps to correct it. It is up to *no one* to bail you out. People need to circulate money. We live in a society that exchanges money for goods and services. It's when spending is greater than earning that it becomes an issue. For the enabler within us, the scariest thing we can do is to say no. We fear we will lose love, respect, admiration, and cause another individual's downfall if we do not step in to help when asked. Set up mechanisms to remind yourself not to get caught up in others' debt. It's a sinkhole.

I save years of bank records reflecting my personal financial history. While this may be weird and a drag on space in the garage, it's important to me. Keeping records showing I paid every single expense for my mother's care for four and half years, has been a good reminder about spending money where it counts, and not blowing it on stupid stuff.

Profit from Performance

Performance earns money. *Innovative* performance earns more because that's when we provide exciting results. To earn more money, look for problems and find solutions to them. If you do something you're good at, energized about, and have a passion for, then share it with as many people as possible. If you're making a difference, it's time to start making money from the difference you make. We each have a unique set of skills and strengths that no one else on this earth has. Find your strengths. Share them, profit from them, and live the life you deserve.

Eliminate Lottery Mindset

The Lottery is not a strategy or a plan. It is a fluke. It's fun to fantasizee about winning. It's a game of chance, designed to profit the organization who governs the program. Parents and in-laws are not a retirement plan. This mindset weakens generations of people. They're robbed of joy that comes as the result of earning their own living. Luck and help is wonderful when we get it, but relying on it is unrealistic.

I believe financial decisions need to be made by all parties who sign the tax return. Be your own lottery ticket. Rely on yourself. Certainly we need others if we're growing something big, but if it's our idea, the buck starts and stops with us.

Teach Kids what "Earning" Means

When children are old enough to understand the calculator on our smart phone, get them using it to manage their own little budget. When they want something, they need to learn it does not fall from a tree or a rich relative.

Gifting our children the opportunity to make decisions about prioritizing how to use their resources, is an important part of a child's well-rounded development. We can start by exchanging chores and tasks for toys, or anything that teaches them to work and earn what they want. These are wonderful lessons they will carry for the rest of their lives.

Allowing our children to take what is not theirs, laughing it off as something cute, tells them this is how life will work. In reverse, never rewarding our children for doing more than we expected (even with a cookie or a hug) could make them stop trying.

Examine your relationship with money, saving, debt, and your family history. Protect yourself where you need to. Contribute your time and your money where you want to make a difference. Teach your children well.

Consider the Following:
- Can you remember back to the first time you earned money?
- What did you do with that money? Spend it? Save it? Give it away?

The things we did as children are typically the way we relate to money as adults.

SUMMARY OF THE FIVE KEY AREAS OF LIFE

In Part 2, we explored the Five Keys of Life Balance. Consciously reviewing these keys on a regular basis, will contribute to our happiness and satisfaction.

Living with integrity, transparency, and intention in every area of life, provides more joy than hanging on to negativity, regrets, or the past ever will.

Cleaning up our mistakes, taking responsibility for our failures, learning and moving forward, frees our mind for better days ahead.

Getting support when we need it, learning how to fortify our shortcomings and living up to our full potential, is incredibly gratifying.

Being a good neighbor and a good humanitarian, leaves a better legacy than sitting idly as life passes us by.

Get creative and make your own lists and charts, fill them with what is important to you and your family. Focus on your big lifetime goals to help narrow down what you allow in and weed out from your life.

For your memory, here are the Five Keys: Physical Being, Relationships, Spiritual Needs, Career and Education, and Personal Finances.

Part Three:
Create Time for Everything

The service industry is chaotic. We arrive at work and hit the floor running. There's the front facing side, where we intersect with clients, and there's the backend, behind the scene where we and our employees put it all in motion. After spending our whole day in this complex work arena, we go home and manage our personal world too!

The complaint about there never being enough time actually creates a feeling like we are the victim to time. All we have is time. It's how we live within the confines of a schedule that predicts our stress regarding time management.

Our family needs to come first. Our professional relationships need to come first. Our friends want to come first and our personal time needs to come first. The list goes on. The one thing in common with everyone needing more of our time...is us.

To manage or waste our time is something we are totally in control of. Living with intention regarding what we accomplish, who we involve and how much we take on, is solely up to us.

When I created the workshop *Yes, There Is Enough Time* in the 1990's, it was in response to numerous people asking how I managed businesses, raised children, ran organizations, traveled weekly, had time for myself, and made it all look easy. There was no secret or magical formula. I had no team of personal assistants picking up after me. I was practical with how I used each hour and each day, to a fault. I managed my time; the clock didn't manage me.

My practical tactics were devised, based on where I lost minutes in each day, and where I felt rushed or stressed along the way. This was a learned process. I had to take an intricate look at everything I was doing in order to calculate what needed to go, what needed to stay, and how to be effective at everything I chose to keep.

Assessing our time use is something we simply don't do. It is the *only* way to improve how we spend it.

Space management is the same. If we assess our kitchen, remove everything we never use, pack holiday or 1x a year items in deeper storage, we suddenly have adequate space. A few years ago, I checked all expiration dates on spices. I still had spices from my mother! I lined them up, took a photo for posterity's sake, and threw them away.

We can find time and space when we make it an exercise to do so. Until we are aware of every little time-taking step in our days, we have no power to arrange our life to function as we need it to. We decide the level of quality for the time we spend with each person or circumstance.

Children remember the focused time we spend with them. They also remember when they feel like our nuisance. I see many young children crying and misbehaving while their mom is on her cell phone, ignoring them. This is a common display of parental neglect, as well as teaching children how much or little respect they should expect in life.

THE ENTREPRENEURIAL TIME SYSTEM®

I mentioned in the "Career and Education" section of the last chapter that I joined Dan Sullivan's *Strategic Coach®* Program. The time I spent there was some of the most productive I've spent in business. Not only did I come up with the ideas that transformed the way gift cards are sold in the beauty industry, I also greatly improved my productivity using less time. One of the first concepts Dan teaches is *The Entrepreneurial Time System*. The *system* consists of splitting time into three parts: Time for Relaxation, Planning, and Money-Making.

The most elegant distinction I got from applying Dan's time system is "setting relaxation first." Meaning, at the beginning of my year I choose which days I'll take off. Most people don't take time for relaxation. They work, then work, and then work more. Even on weekends, they take work phone calls, check social media and emails. They have no uninterrupted time. Their life is their work, and it defines them. There is a contrived badge of honor for working the hardest. I've yet to meet anyone who *started* a business so it could suck the life out of them.

As leaders, our greatest asset is our mind. We need to think creatively to sell better. We need to come up with new, innovative ideas to grow our business. In order to do that, we need our brains to be in top shape.

We all believe free time is something we earn. When we've worked hard enough, and the fatigue has compounded so highly, only then is it time to take a break. However, Dan's mindset is that free time comes first.

Rejuvenation is a precondition for high performance. As a result of personal time away from our business, we come back with fresh ideas and innovations.

Focus Days® are for money-making activities. These days are designed to focus on our short- and long-term cash flow and business growth. Sales appointments, speaking engagements, media appearances, and meetings with top clients are all examples of time spent on revenue production. The tasks that energize us and make us money are *Focus Day* activities.

Buffer Days® are for strategic planning. The purpose of these days is to set up our Focus Days and to make sure we're protecting our time on Free Days®. Dan points out three ways to organize: cleaning up loose ends (admin, financial, legal, etc.), Delegating (team meeting, project prep, reviewing timelines, etc.), and New Capabilities (reading, seminars, skills, etc.).

Those three categories of time have positively changed my whole entrepreneurial experience. Dan's system improved the way I work and changed my personal and family life in a profound way. I highly recommend his book, *The Time Breakthrough*: Transforming Time from a Quantity to a Quality.

ON BEING LATE

Making anyone wait for us is just plain disrespectful. The minutes are gone and they can never be recaptured. When we know we're going to be late, communicate this to all parties involved. When we are late on a regular basis, it's usually due to blind spots when preparing to leave. We look at the clock, think about the time it will take to travel, and then pace ourselves. If we forget to calculate the time to grab keys, our coat, bring the dog in, turn the TV off, or scrape snow from our car, we will be late. If we can start recognizing these blind spots, factor in the time needed, and then add a few extra minutes for insurance, we will arrive at our destination without the stress associated with running late. When one of my businesses was affected by a major construction project, my staff was consistently late. After a few weeks, I suggested they leave for work ten minutes earlier. They simply were blind to the fact they needed to adjust their timing.

HELP OTHERS BE ON TIME

Years ago, I had a fabulous group of clients. They were all high-performing individuals. I loved seeing them. Our conversations were deep and meaningful. There was just one issue. Many of them were late for our appointments. They would call in, a few minutes before their scheduled arrival time. They thought it was ok to be late because they communicated it. I put a sign on the reception desk, *"Please remember: running 'just 10 minutes late' affects your designer and every other client for the rest of the day."* This stopped the problem. Was it harsh? Maybe. In the service industry, mostly what we sell is time. No one wants partial services, but this is what happens when we only allow partial time.

Time management is a learned skill. I was the worst person at it, until "life" forced me to figure it out. See, having children adds a layer of complexity to our timeline (if you're nodding your head, you know what I mean). We must bend to accommodate our children at the rate they can go. My son, Giuseppe, told me one morning when he was around three, "Mom, I can't go as fast as you, I'm too little!" This stopped me in my tracks. I was trying to force him to be faster than he could be, because I was rushed in the mornings. I then started packing his lunch at night, chose his daycare clothes the night before, I woke up an hour earlier and I changed our morning routine. It then became enjoyable, rather than a mad rush to get to work on time.

Managing time is not difficult once we have our priorities in order. It's only when we believe time manages us, that we feel stressed about the clock. Plan mornings to allow enough time for your body clock to work. If you're not a snappy morning person, you may need an extra thirty to forty-five minutes of being awake before you move into action. Know this about yourself. Become more aware of how you manage or mismanage your habits and priorities throughout the day, then adjust the behavior.

Being reasonable is also important. I once had a relationship where time was a big issue. I would say "the trip will take 2 hours; I should arrive about 4:00 p.m." If I encountered traffic and got there at 4:04 p.m., there was an issue. If I arrived at 4:12 p.m., the level of upset usually wrecked the entire night. I accepted the irresponsibility; after all, I *was* late. Time was used as a control mechanism to undermine my equality in the relationship.

We must decide on what is acceptable, and then let others know how much we value our own time when they impinge upon it.

If you have any questions about your conduct with time, please ask your friends and close co-workers. Sometimes we need to hear it from a trusted source. When we are habitually late, we put others under undue stress. Be considerate with yourself and those who your timeliness impacts.

Here are a few suggestions that may be helpful in finding more time:

- Identify blind spots throughout your day.
- Ease up on your mornings with a few simple steps like keeping keys by the door, loading backpacks at night, placing items for transport in your car the night before, and choosing your outfit, shoes and accessories the night before.
- Set a timer on social media or similar distractions that eat away hours of your day.
- While you're waiting for loads of laundry to finish, organize your spice rack, medicine cabinet and cleaning products to be alphabetized for quicker finding.
- Clean closets, removing all items you don't use. This allows you to quickly find what you want.

- Set aside time for yourself every day, even if it means waking up thirty minutes earlier, to focus on the key areas of life that provides balance.
- Schedule specific time to handle issues, problems, and loose ends.
- Schedule dates with your loved ones, doing what you love to do.
- Book vacations, holidays, and romantic trips ahead of time and work around your free time.
- Hire or barter with neighborhood youth or professionals to help with big seasonal tasks and home care.
- Involve your children in all house tasks. They will always live in a house and need to know simple repair tasks. Fixing things together etches great memories and creates fun stories.
- Evaluate if you really need eight hours of sleep, or could you sleep for seven and find an extra hour?
- Sleeping in on weekends, negatively affects our natural rhythm, and wastes hours of fun time.

End each day with only gratitude for everything you actually accomplished!

Devising a Growth Plan

To this point, we've defined our dreams, chosen our vision, taken account of life balance, and created a new perspective of time management.

Attention to personal growth is paramount to eliminating chaos in our company. Control comes from taking specific, intentional, and reasonable steps.

Next, we're going to talk about growing your business.

Cash (Flow) is King

When speaking to groups, I ask: "How many of you want to open a new business so you can make a lot of money?" Lots of people raise their hands. If we're willing to work and are good at what we do, we deserve to earn more money. Yet, we aren't entitled to anything. The only way to grow revenue and profits is by having a solid plan for growth.

One of the most common errors I see *many* business owners make – one that prevents them from sustaining, let alone growing their companies, is not being conscious of the numbers in their business.

Knowing our numbers yields two important benefits. The first is specificity in our growth. When we know the summary of all expenses and how those expenses relate to revenue and profit, we know exactly how much money we can afford for new products, assistance, education, and marketing. The second big benefit to knowing our numbers is less stress. When we have financial blind spots, we feel an undertow of fear and apprehension.

I use the Profit and Loss statement, (P&L) to plan budgets for all expenses. Creating annual monthly graphs, allows us to quickly see from history, the revenue and expense trends. This eliminates surprises. When something is out of character, we can confidently use the information to find out what is going on. Otherwise, we are only guessing.

Let me give you an example using some round numbers here. Say your monthly nut is $20,000. This means you have to earn 20k before you have an extra penny of profit. If you're open five days a week, you must produce $1000 a day to cover basic expenses. If you're not able to cover your daily nut, you'll need to find ways to reduce expenses.

Perhaps you'll start doing things yourself such as bookkeeping, social media posting, cleaning, or whatever it takes to keep your doors open. There is something to be said for knowing how every component of your operation works. If you don't understand it, it's hard to hire anyone and hold them accountable. But, when we're busy with lead generation and operations, we have less time for strategic planning and growth activities.

Scheduling specific time on a regular basis to review numbers is an important part of understanding the reality of your cash flow. To break it down, cash comes in and cash goes out. The ease, of which it flows, is paramount to reduced stress and less chaos.

A lethal mistake is when cash is tight and important corners are cut. This begins as a temporary change. Maybe we opt for a lesser quality product, staffing reductions, advertising, or education cuts. If revenue isn't increased within sixty days, the temporary change becomes regular. We think we have it finely veiled, except everyone else starts seeing it. This is prime time to be taken advantage of. Our fear makes us desperate. Our desperation causes fear. This cycle is a death march on a business. Once due dates are missed and high interest is being charged, it's difficult to recover.

When revenue unexpectedly slows, we need to quickly make adjustments. The recession was a wakeup call. I prepared for a year in advance by hiring Mystery Shoppers and shoring up all areas of client interface. We negotiated better advertising rates and started offering more in-house promotions. I leveraged long term contracts and personal relationships. We brought education back to in-house. I changed utility providers, landscapers, reduced my salary, and put off capital improvements as long as I could. It caused me to find and cut fat wherever I could. I expected an eighteen month downturn. Thirty months in, I felt myself back in 1980, when my client base folded due to the local economy. This was a nauseating time.

What I didn't cut was health benefits, staffing, and anything clients were exposed to. I reduced the amount of advertising, yet kept our brand out there in a few key places. I'll speak more to this in the 'Brand Building' section.

The question becomes, "How do you keep your eye on your numbers in an easy, effective way?" The answer is "Know your P&L Statement."

Know your P&L

The P&L statement is like taking the pulse of a business's finances. It will show, in undeniable terms, if your company is profitable or not. It starts by summarizing revenue and expenses, and reveals the net profitability of your business.

If you're serious about growth, you need to know these numbers like the back of your hand. You don't necessarily need to manually enter any of these numbers. Diligent bookkeepers are priceless. However, it's important you know what the summaries mean, so you can best grow your company making sensible decisions based on financial facts.

There are nine line items you should know on a weekly or monthly basis. They are the following...

1. **Revenue.** All areas of income make up this number. Breaking it down to specific areas, such as: consulting, services, product sales, equipment sales, liquor sales, food sales, or whatever areas you collect revenue from, really helps to see the trends.

2. **Direct Costs.** Also known as the cost of goods sold (COGS). These costs are only related to the cost associated with products and services you offer.

3. **Gross Margin.** This is revenue minus direct costs. This number tells how much money you have after you've covered your direct costs. For instance, if you buy a box of soap for $200, sell it for $300, and then your gross margin would be $100.

4. **Operating Expenses.** These are all other costs associated with your business, except interest on loans and taxes.

5. **Operating Income.** This is also known as *earnings before interest, taxes, depreciation, and amortization* (EBITDA). You calculate this by subtracting your total operating expenses from your gross margin.

6. **Interest.** Any interest payments your company makes on loans.

7. **Depreciation and Amortization.** These are expenses associated with the assets your company holds. Time makes an impact on the value of assets (like telephone equipment, computers, or furnishings, for instance). You will note the expense is of declining value here.

8. **Taxes.** These are any taxes you expect to pay on sales.

9. **Net Profit.** Oh my goodness, finally! These are also known as *net earnings*. After all your hard work, energy, and effort, this is the money your business gets to keep.

My managers and I review these numbers on a regular basis, and always before staff meetings. If something is out of alignment, we discuss what needs to change, as a group.

I don't run a completely open book policy with staff. I have in the past; it's a personal decision for you to make. My technical and support staff might not understand or care about seeing details. I've also learned employees don't have the stomach for seeing red. It scares them. Keeping their confidence level high when things are tight is your role as a leader.

As a whole, we formulate ideas for financial improvement. The sense of ownership people feel when their idea is generating revenue, builds loyalty and pride.

This act alone develops long term employee relationships. They're invested in the financial welfare and success at a more personal level.

I learned how to understand these numbers by bartering services with a CPA when I was nineteen. She taught me bookkeeping, inventory, cash flow, and bank reconciliation, on Tuesday nights. I styled her hair on Friday mornings.

Most creative based business owners say things like "I got into this because I wasn't good at math." None of us need to be good at math. I still pull out a calculator if I'm subtracting something with a lot of zeros.

A Profit and Loss statement isn't math; it is a practical guide which shows us what we need to know to make educated decisions in every category of spending in our company.

Stop Chaos before It Corrupts your Company

When I lost my first business in a building fire, I was underinsured. This is when I learned the value of having a great insurance policy, updating it on an annual basis, and becoming friends with my agent, so I understood how insurance worked.

When we lost all personal possessions in our house fire years later, we were well insured, because of my previous experience. Not needing to worry about money, made an incredible difference in our stress level after a tragic situation. When one of the Spas had a flood a few years later, we lost a year's worth of expensive makeup inventory. We had adequate insurance to cover all cleanup and business interruption. When our home was struck by lightning in 2018, our strong replacement value policy, converted a high stress situation into some paperwork and a big shopping trip.

As my business, knowledge, and confidence grew, I knew nothing would be guaranteed. Always being deeply afraid of losing everything, as revenue grew, I paid things off, as I mentioned. It was a priceless feeling, ensuring the security of my home, or commercial properties, or my car. I wasn't raking in huge bucks when I was paying down debt. I never carried a credit card balance for more than one month. I paid extra on my loans, sometimes only $10 a month, but this saves on interest over the long run.

Things improved greatly once I had a higher purpose than my own income. I was then able to start saving. As an entrepreneur, we can be creative to legally lessen our tax burden. When my sons were six and ten, they came to work with me on Saturdays and during summers. They did laundry, watered plants, picked weeds and ran errands. In exchange, they were on my payroll. This money was directly deposited into the bank, where it was then directly debited to their IRA accounts.

Long term compounding investments build wealth, even when they start out small. When the economic downturn happened, I watched countless service businesses close their doors. 30% of the spa industry was gone by the end of 2009, according to a report I read in Women's Wear Daily.

A large part of my spa business is gift card sales, as I've said. Every December, I expect we will do well. This money is put into a money market account. My banker knows our pattern. I've been pointing it out for years, in case they might forget. It's impossible to borrow money when we don't have collateral. Build collateral before buying extravagant things!

Create a Financial Buffer

Not having safety net money creates intense chaos. Getting co-signers, means we put someone else at risk. Personal co-signers are hard to come by. It's better to make our own financial Plan B. Lines of Credit exist for this purpose.

I secured my first line of credit for $25,000 when I didn't have any intention of using it. When it expired, I secured a new L.O.C for $75,000. When it expired, I secured a new L.O.C for $100,000. I didn't use it for years, uuntil 2010, when the line of credit was the only money I had to keep my company afloat. Use your money to secure lines of ccredit and increase buying power when you have it. When your accounts are getting low, banks are hesitant to make loans.

Getting good legal advice is an area to spend wisely. We don't always need a big firm, but find someone who is good at business law, and meet with them before there ever is a problem. Hiring a lawyer when we're under legal pressure means they have no idea what we're really like. They see the slightly crazed version, and they've not yet learned whether they like us or not. The same goes for our CPA. Understand their approach and ask them to teach you what you don't know. When we withhold information from our CPA, we put a blindfold over their eyes. The only way they can be our ally is by having complete information. Depending on how your company is set up, profit or loss may flow through to you personally.

If we have not kept a good set of records, including every penny of every expense, and every penny of income from every area we are collecting it, they cannot creatively and legally help us.

If you get an IRS audit, when the CPA goes in to represent you, they need all the facts. The IRS digs deeper when they smell a rat. Being prepared for an audit is how I run my businesses. In 1996, I had a random IRS audit. Thankfully, my books were in order and I owed no money, taxes, or fines. The auditor told my CPA, who represented me, that I was a rare case of an owner in a cash industry, who had clean books. This audit was stressful. I was called over twenty times that day to answer questions from the auditor. I could answer every question.

Be prepared for an audit. The IRS will send their dogs after you. I know plenty of flashy and unethical business owners who evaded taxes. They probably felt clever about taking cash under the table, until the IRS cracked down on them and they lost their businesses. When we hide nothing, we never lay awake at night worrying about getting caught hiding it.

As owners, we take more risks than anyone. Until we have not slept on a Monday, afraid we were going to be short for payroll on Friday, we have no idea the stress involved with running a business. When politicians who have no clue what this feels like, want to spend my money, it really irks me.

Build your own income into your expenses. Take care of your personal life but don't be greedy. I have friends who had a very successful consulting business. When the downturn happened, they lost their biggest client. They couldn't pay their rent. Their landlord was allowing them to use the space, rent free, for almost a year. When it started getting testy, she asked for their tax returns. When she saw they were not paying her a penny towards back rent, yet each still taking six figure salaries, she tightened the screws.

Everyone has their own formula for building wealth. Build a great business with a long life-cycle and you will likely have something to sell. Your retirement will be better. It's not what you make, but what you keep, that counts. Build assets for yourself and your family. Help others make money as you're making money. Share your skills, share your time, and share the chaos free life you have designed with those you love!

- Questions for consideration: Do you have a comfortable relationship with your CPA, your lawyer, your insurance agent, and your landlord?
- Where can you cut fat from your expenses?
- Where can you increase spending to get a direct R.O.I. (return on investment)?
- Is your entire staff, including hourly assistants, involved in revenue opportunity planning?
- When you need to make cuts, have you communicated to your team in a way where they feel the importance of your decision?

- Have you hired the best quality professionals to help you grow and protect your business?

The adage holds true, "we get what we pay for." When we cheap out on the cost of professional help, whether it is legal, admin, consulting, vendors, or anyone who affects the function and outcome of our company, we pay more in the end to repair damage unqualified people inflict upon us.

If resources are limited, find a local group in your area who support new entrepreneurs. SCORE is an excellent group, if available. Most universities have programs where they work with you as part of their curriculum. Find a mentor who can give their personal guidance and advice. Find clients you respect and ask for help in the areas they excel in. Our clients love to help us grow. We don't need to know all of the answers, but we must find them, and find them from the smartest people we have access to.

Forming an Advisory Group

During start-up, rapid growth, or any time of significant transition, forming an Advisory Group is a sure way to keep your decisions in line with your desired outcomes.

Ideally, this group would consist of people who are experts in the areas where you lack skill or experience. These experts are serving two purposes: teaching you what you need to know and giving their opinion in your decision making process. This can be a paid group, a group you gift with complimentary products or services you offer, or a volunteer group.

In any case, know what you want from the group before you initiate the formation of a well-rounded source of support. If you're not sure, ask someone whom you trust to help you form this group and deliver the invitations.

When adding my third location, I formed a group consisting of: one of the most astute business men I know, my brother, and an expert in marketing; my nephew, a lawyer; a CPA, and a more casual friend who owns a high-end spa in another city. We spoke at regular times each week. Not all people were on all calls. In exchange, I gifted the group member (or their wife) luxury services in exchange for their time.

I've been a member of the Women's President's Organization since 2001. This group was very helpful to my understanding of properly budgeting expenses through a rapid growth phase.

I've also served for Athena Power Link. This is a brilliant format, designed to help young women as they grow their organizations. These panels consist of experienced entrepreneurs in the areas where strength is needed to grow the business, and fortify the female who has won the opportunity for the panel.

Using an advisory group is helpful for short term and long term growth goals. If this level of formality feels foreign, we can always ask a few respected people to answer a series of questions in one-shot communications. In exchange, offer something that shows your appreciation. This could range from a gift card for a restaurant, to a larger and more opulent gift, depending on their level of input and your level of profit from the recommendation.

Building Your Brand

Once I understood Profit Centers, cash flow, and operating expenses enough to focus on building my brand, this became my mission. When I bought my first salon, I had no idea how to market. Crisis creates creative thinking.

In 1980, the Steel industry in Pittsburgh was collapsing, as I referenced earlier. I was struggling to learn how to operate a business. By the end of my first year, over half of my client base was gone. With no money or knowledge of marketing, the one thing I had, was my ability to connect with clients and do good work.

Relying on my cousin Betsy for help, I reinvented my clientele. She was a nurse at that time, and nurses had steady income. She gave my cards away to her colleagues. I gave away introductory haircuts. Betsy was and still is beautiful, had a great hairstyle, and was a walking commercial for me.

By the end of year two, I was profitable. Now I was interacting with clients I loved and creating enough business to add staff. Clients were coming from miles away and referring their friends! Our price point was reasonable, while our talent was superior.

Providing great value, impressing clients beyond their expectations, consistency, being fair, behaving professionally, and being genuinely nice to people, is the foundation to building a great reputation.

Before opening The Sewickley Spa, I was cautioned by many leaders in the beauty field, that there was no market for a Day Spa in the Pittsburgh region. My gut instincts disagreed.

In order for the general public to understand what a Day Spa was, they needed to own the vocabulary associated with it. I've learned if people cannot pronounce words, they ignore them, as to not look foolish.

When people don't understand a concept, they tend to write it off. Making the words common and the understanding easy for what we sell, in a way the general public understands, and is paramount to growing our brand.

A strong brand includes a great (trademarked) logo, readable font, and usually a name that implies what we offer. When our name doesn't reflect what we do or sell, the tag line must be crystal clear.

Partnering with a graphic artist who embraces our vision is critical here. I've been through many. Three standouts, Erin, Mary and Lindsey, have all helped present my vision to the marketplace. Finding a skilled graphic artist who is pleasant to work with is key to your public image. Get samples from a few before committing to any one graphic artist.

I had a plan, which went like this:

For the first few years, I spent a large amount on our advertising budget, up to 30% of annual revenue, when I was intent on being recognized as an integral part of the regional landscape.

My company was chosen, along with a University, Museum, and Health Care System and 50+ locations Jewelry retailer, for a commercial showcasing our city. This aired on US Air flights arriving to the Pittsburgh International Airport. My plan was working.

Tracking where our buyers come from, is a part of the process. It teaches us where to cut back in future spending campaigns. The disappearance of print has changed this, but we still ask our gift card buyers, as they are paying for their purchase, "May we ask, what made you choose The Sewickley Spa?" (*It's one of many crafted scripts for the desk help*) While the majority of our buyers are now repeat clients, we still hear comments like "40th Street Bridge Billboard", "WDVE" and "Chanel 4 News". We learn what works. We don't guess where we spend advertising money. If we're trying a new area or publication, we bargain over the price, using the potential long term relationship as our leverage.

My overriding goal regarding our brand is this: when people think 'Spa', I want them to think 'Sewickley Spa'. When people think 'gift card', I want them to think 'gift card from The Sewickley Spa'.

Every word, visual, music bed, tone and feel, in every print, radio, internet, billboard, and television ad, is crafted to emotionally reach a potential client.

If I'm not sure which images, colors, or script to use, I take a poll. I find people who are like my potential buyers and ask what speaks to them. If I want to reach young men for Valentine's Day, I look for groups of young men to ask which ad would make them buy a gift card for their girlfriend. I've gone so far as to approach a table of men at a bar, showing them samples of three ads (*I happened to be having lunch with my graphic artist and a media buyer in the establishment*). I bought them a round of drinks as a thank-you, and we had our answer. It never fails, the next day, at least one of the strangers I approached with this technique, calls to buy something from us. They tell our receptionist the story. The fact that strangers are left with a funny story, compels them to further talk about us....helping to build our brand.

Know Your Buyers and Your Users

The decision makers are not always the end users. Often, it's a purchasing department decision, with no emotion involved. When this is the case, it's imperative to differentiate what you offer from competitors. Do you offer additional video training once a week for a period of time? Do you provide on-site support? Do you provide recognition and introductions for the end user? Whatever it is, make it clear, make it known, and make it different.

We reach out to two sets of buyers. Women make up 75% of our client base. Men make up 95% of our gift card purchases. For a few years after starting SpaEdge, which I referred to as my fourth and virtual location, I wondered if I was really in the gift card selling business with the spa being our mere fulfillment center.

When you think about your position and your brand, what do you know for sure, and what do you need to learn? Market research companies provide this service if you need assistance.

- Are you clear on the demographic of your client?
- Does your advertising answer questions and remove doubt via the message/visuals/colors?
- Do people know what sets you apart from your competitors by your advertising message?

When we are emotionally connecting to our clients, we craft messages which speak directly to the buyers' wants and needs. If creative advertising is not your thing, hire a professional who fully gets the message you want to share.

There are many great firms, ranging in size and price, which specialize in doing what I am describing here. Media buying can be costly. You must know what you're doing, or you can end up in debt, with money wasted in the wrong place. I've been at it for decades, but I've used a media buyer when dealing with a personal crisis. Susan taught me a lot, but mostly she kept things smooth when I was consumed with caring for an elderly couple who took my attention away from my company for several months.

Marketing is one of my favorite activities. I look ahead at what the market could be excited about. I think about images which promote my ideas. I write compelling scripts for commercials.

When I get stuck, I'll open a book or magazine and pick a word or an image, any word I can find, and I'll build a story around this word that relates to what we offer. When we are clear on what our clients need, we can build a spa story around a pair of boots.

I pay zero attention to what my competitors are doing. When I leaf through publications, our award-winning ads are beautiful and recognizable. Even if people never read the ad, our brand is quickly imprinted in their memory. This is the importance of a great logo and consistent font style.

Imitation is the highest form of flattery, until it confuses the innocent public. I've had many 'cease and desist' letters written to imitators who copy our ads. Even a desperate competitor once was caught hijacking our website searches. This is illegal diversion. This unscrupulous profiteer was stealing our internet search clients. Karma looms over unethical individuals. Skilled IT people now monitor our sites.

Make Your Policies Widely Known and Respected

If clients have not been thoroughly educated on our policies, they cannot be expected to abide by them. For service businesses, the parameters of the contracts, the policies, and the guidelines, are all we have to protect us. Sharing this information with every person the policy affects is critically important. Our lawyer has reviewed all written, stated, and shared policies. This step alone, makes upholding them important. There were a number of years when our cancellation policy was included in every written advertisement. I never wanted the public to feel like we were bamboozling them when we had to uphold it.

When a policy isn't upheld, by anyone who represents us, they set a precedent that the policy can be broken. This is costly to any company.

As for employment policies, they also need to be clear, concise, thorough, understood, and agreed to in writing. When an employee breaks a policy, there must be an incident report written and placed in the employee file. Documentation, even for the simplest infringements, is cardinal.

When something out of the ordinary happens with a client or an employee, the details need to be captured immediately. Even by the next day, our memory tricks us into believing what we want to believe, and forgetting the accurate details.

A perfect example of this happened last year. We had an employee making terroristic threats in one of my businesses. I was a few hours away, gathering facts over the phone. I contacted the local sheriff and reported from my notes. I requested all involved parties to write down every detail that happened before they left the building. I was assured this would be done. It wasn't. Months later, when the case went before a local judge, no one could remember exactly what happened. My notes, taken from their words, couldn't even be confirmed. As a result of improper documentation, we were ill-prepared and the perpetrator got a slap on the wrist.

You'll want to document every detail: every 'ten minutes' late for work; goofy email; client complaints; broken policy; or infraction. That documentation saves tremendous time and money in Unemployment Compensation Suits. You'll set yourself up to win cases by being well-prepared, with detailed documents. Staff knows who in management keeps documents and who doesn't. UC costs can cramp cash flow. Protect your company, your reputation, and your clients by having strong, legal policies in place. Ensure everyone understands why policies exist. Require for all policies to be upheld.

- Do you have clear and legal policies in place?
- For both clients and staff?
- Have you fairly and clearly shared these policies and expectations?

Affiliate Partnerships

Using large employers, large events, and out of the box thinking, giving away gifts significant enough to catch attention, but leaving room to earn a profit, is an ideal way to build a pipeline of business. There is an entire industry based around promotional material. Make sure yours is what folks really want to walk away with.

We've been in an affiliation with the largest employer in the city for over a decade. We provide a beautiful $25 digital gift card for their website, which employees print and redeem. We extend the offer for up to one guest. This simple gift has been a great source of new clients. And better yet, the water fountain banter is about my company!

- Where can you give away gifts to gain reputation and clients?
- What relationships can you leverage to grow your brand?

The Face of Your Company

People trust a product or a company when they attach a person to the brand. Think Oprah, Microsoft, Dr. Dre Beats. There is a sense of transparency and deeper connection when a personality we know a little bit about is involved. When there's someone to personally relate to, the connection is deeper.

Positioning our products and services, not only happens from advertising and promotion, but from live and televised events.

After 911, I went to the site of the Shanksville crash, not far from one of my locations. I ran into Mike Clark, a local TV celebrity and friend through our children's school. I asked Mike to help me gain security clearance to send a team of massage therapists to perform chair massages on the emergency responders. Hundreds of people were working double shifts in grueling circumstances.

My staff members were thrilled at the opportunity to help. They refused to be paid for their time to go every day before or after work to help at the wreckage site. We did this out of concern for our country, in a time where we all united in the most healing way I've witnessed in my lifetime.

We never did this for recognition, but for the next few years, the contribution of my company was a very positive and helpful conversation in the community.

Supporting non-profits we care about, is also an appreciated and charitable way to make great connections while making our presence known. When people are passionate about a charity, they tend to support the establishments that support their cause. Make it easy by making your company a dependable and notable supporter of what you care about.

Local media coverage is great. Being in the national and international media, positions us as innovative leaders in the field. We can meet people in the locker room, the

airport, or while on vacation. Always having your story
ready, and something printed or tangible to make a deeper
impression, leads to unexpected opportunities.

Years ago, during an annual conference in New York, I
started chatting with a man while perusing a private-label
skin care booth. We were hitting it off, agreeing on
numerous issues in the beauty industry. I was surprised by
his vast knowledge and ability to communicate so
effectively. As it turned out, he was the owner of the
Audrey Morris Company. Audrey, his mother, was an
innovator in the skin care and cosmetics industry. Wayne
grew the company to the next level, using non-traditional
formulas. That day, due to nothing more than genuinely
enjoying and respecting each other, we entered into a
handshake deal that lasted for many years.

Through this affiliation, we were featured as the cover
story for *Spa Management Magazine.*

We never know who is watching, who we are reaching,
or who is making a decision to do business with us.
Presenting ourselves and our staff as the most professional,
logical choice, is deeply important to securing the positive
image of our company.

People don't want to do business with us when
something is viewed as false or contrived. This ranges from
wearing fake diamonds or knockoff handbags, to making
false claims of results.

Our image causes people to form an immediate opinion about us and what we represent. We never get a second chance at a first impression. Presenting ourselves and our staff for the audience we want to attract is an important part of image building. Clothes don't have to be expensive to look great.

Do you see areas where you can expand your presence? Anywhere people gather is a great place to start.

- Where could you position your company and gain respect and recognition in an unconventional market?
- Have you conditioned your staff to respond properly to questions?
- When tragedy strikes, how can your company help?
- Use the good deeds you do, to create appropriate talking points for your employees to share with clients. These pride points are priceless!
- Craft scripts carefully. We never want to exploit a sad situation. Remember, what people don't know, they tend to make up. Review what staff shares on a regular basis.

Always have something concrete to leave with people. Your photo on your business card makes more of an impression than a run of the mill card that gets tossed in a pile!

Two Types of Business Model

Every business has a cycle. Some are long and steady. Some are brief and brilliant. If you want to build a job, then brief and brilliant may be your thing. If you want to build a company with sustainability and opportunity for growth, slow and steady always wins.

For the trendy business, if you're young and not sure what you want to do in ten years, but want to make a lot of money riding a wave, jump on board! I had tanning beds when they were hot. I made a lot of money with this trend. They're now taboo. I've sold spray tanning, and it's the same thing. I've passed on false lashes, goldfish pedicures, dermabrasion machines, hyperbaric chambers, salt caves, and am currently passing on eyebrow tattooing. There is a business for everyone, as long as there is a market for what is offered.

MAXIMIZING TRENDY GOLD MINES

Fads are great, until they're not. Something new will come along and nudge every hot trend away. If I had bought the microdermabrasion machine I was seriously considering eighteen years ago, I'd still be paying for the machine while dusting it once a week. I decided not to buy it for a few reasons; I'm not a doctor, I don't employ a dermatologist, machines can damage people's skin, and I didn't want the liability.

However, If I wanted to open a glass blowing shop, I would learn everything possible, hire skilled people, buy the best equipment and inventory, go to Venice and learn how the masters do it, create a story around this trip, develop a cool logo, expose myself as the expert in the field, do demonstrations for groups I want to target, and lastly, make a YouTube page and run with it. If I still had this business in seven years, I likely would have made money. Even though the fad would have ended, I'd have resources from riding the wave, which I could use to launch the next hottest idea. This business model can be great.

What isn't great, is when you go to a show, get caught up in the sales pitch, get into debt, are not equipped to perform, sell or teach the service, have no marketing budget, are not properly insured, and the promise to triple your money, never comes to fruition.

MAXIMIZING A GOLDEN GOOSE

Clients want great service. Clients will believe in you if you are good and consistent. Please, don't diminish your value by aligning yourself with anyone or anything whose reputation is not equal to or above yours.

If your intention is to build a well-branded, well-attended and well-respected company, you would go about this with detailed care and planning. Most people start a business because they love what they do and usually had a bad boss in a previous job. Competing with your employer by performing the same services at a lesser price outside of their business is ruthless and unethical. If you want to compete, become competent. Get licensed, inspected, bonded, insured, and pay taxes on your revenue.

Once you decide to open a reputable establishment, choose your core talents, services, and offerings, perfecting this until you are skilled and comfortable enough to expand to the next area of expertise. If you operate during a learning curve in front of clients, you will set your reputation back and likely struggle. Know your craft. Know what you're good at. Know what you're weak with. Supplement your weaknesses with credible people who are better at it than you are. As you grow, delegate the tasks that do not make the company money. Your draining task is another person's dream task. Let it go, but keep accountability present.

Be Referable

You'll grow your business by diversifying your services conservatively with skill and foundation, along with being genuinely pleasant. Gain reputation by offering great service. Showcase your work through social media. Give your clients a reason to share their results with others. Reward them when they do. Position yourself as the leader in the industry by sharing what you know at every opportunity.

Being referable is one of the most important attributes you or your business will ever have. Your brand doesn't grow when you haven't prepared yourself to deliver services reliably and consistently. Your brand suffers when you surround it with unprofessional people. Great people are hard to come by. Train good people to be great people by investing in their training, even if you invest your own time to train them.

Keep it Clean

I cannot stress enough the importance of running a clean operation. Cleanliness breeds trust. Dirt and disorganization breeds mistrust. I'm only on-site in my businesses a few days a month. When I arrive unannounced and the facilities are clean, everyone gets acknowledgement. If I arrive at a hectic time and see or sense there is stress, I roll up my sleeves and start doing dishes, replacing toilet paper rolls, and straightening magazines in the reception room.

If you have a cleanliness issue, it's an opportunity for more training. Deal with it on the spot if it's appropriate. Sometimes it will only take picking up a broom, for others to see what they had previously glazed over.

Looking at our business from the perspective of our clients, should be a regular occurrence. Sit where they sit. Use the restrooms. Notice what they notice. Park where they park and walk in all doors. Have employees do the same thing at least once a month. Visit your own website, call your answering service. Smell it, hear it, and see it. Everyone, including admin, laundry attendants, porters, assistants, etc., should see your business through the eyes of your guests. Leadership makes or breaks this habit.

When everyone is on board with our vision, because we have shared it clearly and positively, there is great culture. Great culture is apparent, when the same thing happens whether *we* are there or not.

Habits for Success

Embracing who we fundamentally are and how we function, is necessary to find life balance. Developing steps to keep our time organized enough to grow our business while enjoying personal time, is valuable.

Developing good habits and ceasing bad habits is a huge step in eliminating chaos.

These are some important habits which help me streamline daily routines. I hope some of them help you.

- Make lists of what needs to be done the next day/week/month.
- Do the most challenging items on the list first.
- Prioritize lists to align with weekly, quarterly, annual, and lifetime goals.
- Allow adequate time with buffers on each end of each task.
- If something lingers at the end of the day, no worries – add it to tomorrow's list and enjoy the evening.
- Identify and notify people in advance, when they are needed.
- Clean the house, mentally and physically.
- Clean and organize the closets.

- Color-code your wardrobe. Seeing a crescendo of color is incredibly helpful when looking for that specific blue shirt.
- Donate or share items that don't fit.
- Organize the bathroom, pitch all expired items responsibly.
- Pitch all makeup, skin care, and toiletries no longer in use, regardless of the label or original cost.
- Organize the kitchen in a way that is ergonomically comfortable.
- Alphabetize the spice rack.
- Pack up, store, or donate rarely used kitchen items to clear up more space on the counters and inside the cabinets.
- Have your kids, spouse, or friends help with major house projects.
- Schedule one big cleaning/organizing project each season.
- Clear the desk of all clutter except the present project.
- Eliminate distractions.
- Clean the car as if the best client is going to be the passenger.
- Balance personal checkbooks, debit cards and bank accounts each month.

- Schedule Doctor/ eye/dental/exam appointments a year in advance.
- Find excellent babysitters who play cool sports and study different languages.
- Help kids transition when they meet new people. Kids often feel hesitant and frightened about meeting people for the first time.
- Have kids help with laundry, dishes, cooking, etc. These could be their best childhood memories.
- Schedule date nights with partner and friends.
- Notice what is admirable in people and randomly share.
- Volunteer one time a month.
- Take kids along, teaching them to give back too.
- Spend time in every part of business where clients and staff spend time. Look through their eyes.
- Conduct regular meetings, begin with gratitude shares. Use teamwork to build plans, make changes and get feedback.
- Schedule uninterrupted sessions, alone or with key people, at least three times a year to focus on growth.
- Ask for feedback, perhaps anonymously at first.

- Question why issue/person/politics/beliefs, cause emotional reaction.
- Discipline clearly, firmly, and respectfully.
- Stretch your mind and body every day.
- Set goals that align with long term plans.
- Wake up in gratitude.
- Reflect on positive parts of the day before sleep.

Rapid growth, whether in personal or business life, can be a grand balance. Set and follow your own guidelines.

Review the questions in this book. Use them as the catalyst to initiate change where you want it and growth where you see it's possible. Use what you considered here to eliminate things that do not serve you. Make your lifelong goals the basis of what you do and don't do. Having your bigger picture, and your higher purpose, keeps it all in perspective.

Eliminating chaos is the key to a sustainable company, free of corruption and disruption. This sense of calm imparts peace and happiness in our daily life. Peacefulness and clarity in our vision leads to prosperity. Prosperity leads to positively impacting the future. The larger our impact, the better our world.

May you streamline your success!

Sincerely,

Dorothy

Additional Resources

TheStrategicCoach.com

JoelBauer.com

Landmarkeducation.com

MarshallGoldsmith.com

JohnjFenton.com

@jefffaldalen

Adherents.com

FormulaMarketer.com

About The Author

One word best describes Dorothy Andreas:

"Committed."

... Committed to entrepreneurs embracing their inner confidence and entrepreneurial spirit. This led Dorothy, as she was putting herself through college in 1980, to abandon school and open her first salon business at the age of nineteen.

Dorothy built a successful model with her first business. This business was lost in a fire in 1984. She quickly reopened in a new location. She expanded with another location and new operating model in 1986. Her success was founded on a reputation for quality service, artistic offerings, and a comfortable environment for clients.

In 1989, with a thriving business, she knew she needed to give something back to her profession. She started "The Possibilities for Success"© seminar, and took this to young people throughout the region, touting the benefits of the beauty industry to teenagers in unfortunate situations. Dorothy stated, "Young people don't often have skills or support to realize they are capable of amazing things. Through sharing my own story, I create the possibilities they may not know exist for themselves." Dorothy has been an advisory board member to beauty schools, guest teacher, lecturer, and mentor for over thirty years. Her focus is ensuring that students are equipped for healthy futures in the beauty profession as well as the business world.

Dorothy's commitment to giving back to her community was evidenced as she was nominated and elected in 1991 to preside over the Business Persons Association of Regent Square. She was the first woman to hold this position. During her terms, the area was transformed to a popular destination, developing a synergy amongst neighbors, merchants, and patrons. Regent Square still benefits from her positive implementations. Dorothy also served as the Vice- President of the Sewickley Chamber of Commerce in 2003-2004.

It was her diplomatic personality, professionalism, and high energy attitude that landed her an invitation to join the Pittsburgh Chapter of The Art & Fashion Group International. In 1994, she was presented with the Master of the Craft Award from the group, in recognition for her artistry and professionalism. Dorothy Andreas quickly gained the confidence of her peers and was elected as the Chapter President. Within months, she implemented many new ideas that were being duplicated throughout the country. By mid-year, the Pittsburgh Chapter had increased membership and funds, to be greater than any of the other 64 Chapters in the organization. The following year, she was elected as the first woman and youngest ever, to preside over "The A&FG." She quickly gained respect and cooperation from her peers and the Art & Fashion Group International had its most successful year to date.

Committed to superior service and products for her clients, as well as the members of the A&FG, Dorothy formed NEDCO, North East Distribution Company, which imported skin and hair products that were new to the United States. She also served as a Director of Education for the company, based in Parma, Italy.

Dorothy is extremely proud of starting the "Annual Cut-A-Thon", an event to raise money for children in homeless situations. Allegheny Intermediate Unit and The Light of Life Mission were the recipients of the funds. The program was replicated in various other chapters of the A&FG, raising in total over $100,000 for charities.

Managing a successful business, raising two young children, while overseeing the operations of the Art and Fashion Group, Dorothy noticed the growing attention of others asking how she managed it all. This led her to develop a unique and informative presentation called "Yes,

There is Enough Time" ©. The workshop, taught nationally to business owners and employees, shifting the idea of time management from something unattainable. Participants gain skills to move from overload to business control and personal joy.

Dorothy Andreas went on to begin organizing and hosting W.I.L.L. seminars, [Women in Leadership League©] a national organization of professional women which deal with personal and career advancements of its members. Aware of a rapidly changing world, W.I.L.L. embraced the philosophy of women being the most integral part of the management, business strategy, and beauty pioneers in their profession. W.I.L.L. gained recognition for outstanding women with skills and knowledge, but lacking appropriate appreciation. Dorothy's determination brought awareness to the women behind the scenes, who have shaped the beauty industry.

Accomplishments

In 1995, Dorothy Andreas, as the first American from the beauty industry, received the "Golden Scissors Award" from the Columbian Beauty Association. Her efforts to bring recognition to this group, proves evident, as through her work, Columbians are now graciously invited to perform in American Productions in the beauty industry.

Also, in 1995, Dorothy Andreas co-produced and emceed "The World Masters" show in New York, hosting beauty professionals from sixty-four countries.

In 1996, Dorothy Andreas co-produced "L'Evente Globale", the industry's first educational show to be held in Europe by an American concern. The event, attended by over 1,500 beauty professionals from four continents, was held in the resort town of Rimini, Italy. Later that year, she received the "President's Award" from the A&FG International, for outstanding commitment to her profession.

On March 10, 1996, at a gala dinner in New York City, Dorothy was presented with the "Founders Award." Three hundred beauty leaders from thirty-five countries gave her a standing ovation for her many contributions to the beauty industry.

In 1998, Dorothy opened The Sewickley Spa, a regional destination spa nestled in the charming village of Sewickley Pa.

In 2001, Dorothy opened The Sewickley Spa at Ligonier Pa, and in 2003, The Sewickley Spa at the Wisp Resort in Deep Creek Maryland.

In 2016, along with partners, Dorothy opened The Greene Turtle, a seafood-based sports bar in Deep Creek,

Maryland. Dorothy serves as the Operating Partner for this location.

The Pittsburgh Business Times and Bizjournals, recognized The Sewickley Spa as one of the 'Top 100 Fastest Growing Businesses" from 2001-2004.

In 2003, Governor Ed Rendell recognized Dorothy Andreas as one of Pennsylvania's "Best 50 Women in Business".

In 2004, Dorothy founded SpaEdge Inc, the first technology company to offer online printable gift cards for the beauty industry. This innovative concept, transformed the beauty industry by reducing costs and enhancing convenience for both spa owners and users.

In 2006, The Winners Circle of Westmoreland County; Seton Hill University, YWCA and Westmoreland Chamber of Commerce, presented Dorothy with "The Entrepreneurial Excellence Award", for positively impacting the business community in Westmoreland County, mentoring young women, and setting an example of professional business standards.

In 2007, Dorothy launched EGiftTech.com, a service for retail websites to offer instantly printed gift cards to their clients.

In 2012, Dorothy was the recipient of the "Top 25 Most Influential Women" award from the Pittsburgh Business Times.

Dorothy is a recent past member of the board of The Dove Center and Shelter for victims of domestic and sexual abuse. Under her two terms as Board Chair, the agency secured funding for a 1.4M shelter. Dorothy was the 2009-13 President of the Western Maryland Health Planning Council, St Mark's Lutheran Church Council President from 2010-2016, Founding Member; Garrett County Steps to Better Health and Garrett County Annual Health Fair. She has served on Western Md chapter of the Red Cross Board of Directors, Commission for Women, Garrett County Memorial Hospital Foundation, and she was active at a Board level with the Deep Creek Lake Sailing Association. In 2016, she and her husband, Daryl, chaired The Force. This group raised 1.9M in nine months to provide funding for a new life saving Cancer Care Center at GRMC.

Dorothy has been an active member of Women Presidents Organization since 2001. Dorothy has also participated for many years at various times with The Strategic Coach[TM], Landmark Education[TM], and is a graduate of Joel Bauer's Mentoring 4Millions[TM].

Dorothy currently resides in Pennsylvania, Maryland and Georgia, with her husband, Daryl T Walters. Daryl has served the Maryland State Judicial System for over twenty years, while doing charitable work through Rotary Club, Commission for Women, Dove Sexual Abuse and Rape Crisis Center, and Whitetails Unlimited, among other concerns. They are the proud parents of Ashley, Giuseppe, Julian, and their beloved pets. She oversees the operation and growth of the Sewickley Spa Inc. and The Greene Turtle Deep Creek. Dorothy is a speaker, writer, teacher of Cosmetology, mentor, and an avid supporter of women's rights, animal rights and the homeless.

For more information, visit...

www.DorothyAndreas.com

Made in the USA
Columbia, SC
17 February 2019